The
MBA
Application
ROADMAP

The Essential Guide to Getting into a Top Business School

**Stacy Blackman
and
Daniel J. Brookings**

Port
www.

D1343533

Cover and interior design by Masha Shubin
Cover photo 2008 © René Mansi. Image from iStockPhoto.com

www.firstbooks.com

ISBN-13 978-0-912301-89-1
ISBN-10 0-912301-89-9

Publisher: First Books
First Books® is a registered trademark of FirstBooks.com, Inc.

Printed in the U.S.A.
All paper is acid free and meets all ANSI *standards for archival quality paper.*

Rev1

Table of Contents

"Tales from the Road" are dispersed throughout this book, offering up various perspectives on a wide array of personal experiences. These are real quotes from real people who have been willing to share a bit of their experiences with us. While the authors do not necessarily agree with each and every sentiment offered here, every one of these clients was successful, clear evidence that the process is not black and white. There are as many approaches as there are types of people, and certainly more than one route can lead to success.

Introduction

From Stacy

When I applied to business school in 1996, I knew exactly what I wanted to do with my life and thus with my MBA education: transition from a number-crunching financial analyst into a brand manager at a consumer products company, managing brands like Crest toothpaste and Nestle Crunch candy bars. I was thrilled when I was admitted to my first choice school, Kellogg—the number one MBA program for marketing in the world. Once school started, I excitedly joined the marketing club, attended every marketing event on campus, and during recruiting for summer internships, I interviewed with all of the top companies. Once again, I saw my dreams fall into place: I landed a summer internship working on Pillsbury's Häagen Dazs brand. Unfortunately, when I started my internship, things did not go as planned—I did not enjoy the internship and seriously wondered if brand management was really the right fit for me.

When school started again in the Fall, I went into a panic—I was one half of the way through my business school experience and I had to start from scratch—I had no idea what I wanted to do with my life.

But it was then that the true magic of business school revealed itself. I opened my eyes and started to consider all of the possibilities and opportunities that were right in front of me: incredible, interesting, ambitious students; brilliant and accessible professors; clubs; conferences; lectures; parties; travel opportunities; and plenty of time to experiment. By the time I graduated, I had founded a company with two classmates, received a term sheet from a prominent investment fund, sold the company to a much larger one in San Francisco, and had been profiled by *Fortune* magazine for this adventure. All in nine short months. For many people business school is about landing the dream job at McKinsey or Goldman Sachs or General Mills. But I believe for everyone the true benefit of business school is in the possibilities that it presents. What I did in business school and have done since was not even in my "consideration set" before. Business school opened my mind, bolstered my confidence to pursue bigger dreams, and gave me tools to pursue them. Not to mention, it was a ton of fun!

Having run an MBA Admissions Consulting company since 2001, I derive great satisfaction from working every day with clients to help them gain this experience, and help set them on the path to accomplish their ambitious goals and become great leaders.

The goal of our company is to help clients be successful and to do so with a bit less stress. I am often asked what books an applicant should purchase to serve as a reference throughout the process. When I look at most of the offerings, they are 500-plus pages—not exactly an easy read for someone who is juggling the GMAT, application essays, and a full-time job. The goal of our book is to distill down the key points that we believe you need for the process, and to present you with them in a simple and easy format. I believe that the information within this book contains the true basics of what you need to know, and better yet, is light enough to take on a plane and short enough to read on the plane. Daniel and I wanted to create a book that, when read straight through at the beginning of your process, will give you a great overview of the entire application process. But, we wanted the content to be specific enough about the different phases that you can refer back to it when you are sitting down to write that leadership essay or getting ready to prep your recommenders.

My passion for marketing never subsided—marketing is what I do every day with our clients, just in a form that I never expected. I market people to their dream schools, rather than market ice cream to people. Throughout the book you will see how marketing is an essential part of this process and my hope is that you can become an effective personal marketer before you even set foot on a business school campus.

Wishing you much success,

Stacy Blackman

From Daniel

Welcome to the wonderful world of MBA applications. Whether you are a "lone wolf," applying on your own, or are surrounded by hordes of friends and colleagues scrambling throughout the holiday season because round 2 deadlines are approaching, this can be a harrowing and all-consuming experience. Your days and nights can disappear, swallowed by endless cycles of spellchecking and grammar-checking.

Or this can be a reasonably fun and fulfilling time where you look at all of the opportunities you have in front of you and take stock of your achievements to date. Stacy and I hope you decide to view it as the latter. We wrote this book as a guide for the optimistic people who want to showcase their hard work, intelligence, leadership, and creativity in order to join some amazing educational communities.

This isn't a book designed to help people "game the system." Stacy and I are both proud alums of MBA programs and have too much respect for our alma maters to create that sort of guide. Rather, we hope this can be a resource that lets people from all types of backgrounds better assess and then explain the kinds of talents and experiences that will make them valuable to an MBA community. Many MBA aspirants come from places like top consulting firms and elite investment banks. But great applicants come from all types of backgrounds, and some "non-traditional" candidates don't fully comprehend how valuable their knowledge and experiences can be to an MBA community. I have to tell you, a lot of the classmates I learned the most from were running small businesses or working for not-for-profits or developing new technologies or patrolling under the waves in a sub the year before they showed up at HBS. I hope this can be a valuable guide for the full spectrum of applicants, from the investment banker writing essays between IPOs to the naval lieutenant assembling his apps under 1000 feet of water.

MBA applicants have a great opportunity to use this process not just as a period to grind out a bunch of applications, but as a time for productive self-reflection about life goals and a chance to improve oneself. This is a great time to take inventory about priorities in our careers, families, and lives as a whole. I'm truly impressed by the young adults—usually three to four years into their careers—who take advantage of the opportunity to review their progress to date and who seek out the feedback and overall counsel of mentors, co-workers, family members, and friends.

This can also be a period used for self-improvement in important areas, particularly in an area near and dear to my heart: writing. Let's face it, young adults starting their careers these days more often than not see their writing skills deteriorate pretty quickly. Writing emails, IMs, text messages, and bulleted slides in PowerPoint all day will do that to a person. But good writing can be a valuable tool in a post-MBA business career. People who pay attention to careful wordcraft, storytelling, and organization during this process won't just have a leg up for admissions, they will have hopefully rebooted their writing abilities.

We know you look at the task in front of you and believe it's a long hard slog. But we also hope you can embrace the opportunity and have a good time with it—at least a relatively good time.

Cheers, and best of luck.

Daniel J. Brookings

Is Business School Right for You?

CHAPTER 1

Do You Really Want or Need This Degree?

I **regularly receive inquiries from** MBA applicants who desperately want to go to business school, in fact they want to go to X school…and only want to know: how can we make that happen for them immediately? They are focused on a very specific and ambitious goal, but as we probe a bit deeper and discuss post-MBA goals, their personalities, and more, we come to question whether the MBA is actually the right next step.

Many people feel that the MBA is the cure-all. It's what your friends are doing, it's what your parents want you to do, it's what you can do until you figure out what you really want to do! As you venture down the road of business school applications, it is certainly easy to fantasize about the name of that big MBA program eventually appearing on your resume and how it will open any door you want. However, the MBA is not the end game, it's just a means to an end, and certainly can be a very effective tool if used well and if appropriate for you.

One fairly easy way to determine if the MBA is right for you is to take stock of your short- and long-term goals and figure out if the MBA will truly be an asset in helping you to get there. Admissions committees will certainly be asking this question and one of the easiest ways to receive a "ding" is to discuss a set of goals that are just not applicable to an MBA degree. For example, perhaps you should be pursuing a degree in accounting, arts management, or law.

Of course there are many people who do not know exactly what they want to do. Because the MBA is a flexible degree, it can appeal to an individual who wants to take a little break, reassess, and then jump back into his or her career. Surely, citing more ambiguous reasons such as leadership training and an extended network is justified. But not everyone really wants to be a leader, and not everyone needs an impressive network in the business world. Be honest with yourself as you consider your goals.

As you determine whether an MBA program is right for you, it is important to be realistic about what an MBA program can provide. This is different for everyone. For some it may be a chance to interview on campus with a dream company. For some it may be the credibility it brings to your resume when you go to raise money for a new venture. For others it may be the opportunity to learn functional skills required to effectively run a business. Be honest about what you are seeking from the MBA and decide whether it can really provide what you need. This is a good time to do general research, network with business school students and alums, and speak with individuals in your target career. Find out what they think of the MBA experience. Decide if the experience they are describing sounds like a good fit for you.

Because there is no checklist of reasons for wanting the MBA, and because the MBA can be valuable in so many different functions and roles, this can be a confusing step. I find that many people know in their hearts whether they really want the MBA. Frequently, when applicants aren't truly excited about pursuing an MBA, they just are not driven to work hard; they procrastinate on GMAT prep and dawdle on their essays. It's a long and expensive process, and certainly not worth it if it does not make sense for your goals or personality. Plus, the admissions committees will likely be able to smell your indecision and your application will then be unsuccessful.

After you prove to yourself that you want an MBA, you may be surprised to find that there are many different audiences who want to understand "why?".

CHAPTER 2

"Why Do You Want to Go to Business School?": Multiple Constituencies, Multiple Answers

You're going to be asked that question a lot over the next several months, so you need to come up with a good answer. Actually, several different good answers, each tailored for distinct constituencies.

MBA admissions boards: Show them that you appreciate the value of learning opportunities and have taken advantage of them. Illustrate how the MBA program will be a better place to develop your skills and further your interests than your current job or even your likely next job would be.

Colleagues/managers: There are many firms where young professionals regularly exit to attend MBA programs, and a fresh crop of MBAs cycles in every fall. In other workplaces, some colleagues might view an exit as "giving up on the team." You don't want your MBA admission to cast a pall over your final months in your current job. If you explain your MBA as a tool to prepare yourself for opportunities a decade or two down the road—rather than as a route to get a better job than you could get coming from your current position—they may be more supportive.

"The Doubters": Last year, a couple of my clients recounted how alumni interviewers probed deeply on why they were applying, even going so far as to say to an entrepreneurially inclined individual, "You don't need an MBA to do what you want to do." Candidates who may want to stay in the same field (or return to the same firm) after graduation and those who want to enter the not-for-profit or government sectors often hear the same stuff. My would-be-entrepreneur candidate was prepared: she countered with a list of a half dozen world-renowned entrepreneurs from this particular MBA program.

"Da Haters": There are people who don't see the value of business school at all (shocking…shocking, I know). After all, business people usually don't need accreditations like doctors, lawyers, and some other professionals. You should be prepared to talk about why this will not just be a "two-year vacation" for you.

CHAPTER 3

Am I Too Old (or Too Young)?

Ten years ago, the question on everyone's mind was, "Am I too young?" Back then, the more experience the better...the older the better...

More recently, top schools such as Stanford and Harvard have stated that they are taking a closer look at younger candidates, and are even willing to admit candidates with no work experience. One reason behind this was that some candidates may be so successful two to three years out of school that they would not consider going back at that point. Thus, the schools would be missing an opportunity to admit some exceptional talent. Some applicants are just plain ready right out of college. A few have started and/ or run a business in school, participated significantly in a family business, or gained applicable experiences via other avenues. They have focused goals, are personally mature, and are truly ready to take the plunge. Yes, some of these schools are opening their eyes more to less experienced candidates, but this does not mean that younger candidates overall have a better chance of success.

Younger candidates will have their fair share of challenges. They will need to work harder to prove that they possess the focus, confidence, and maturity necessary to excel in an MBA program. They will also need to prove that they have enough insights and experiences to be a contributing member of the student population. Being a subscriber to the *Wall Street Journal* since first grade will only get you so far; personal experiences are far more valuable to other students' classroom experiences. Finally, younger applicants will need to convince the admissions committee that they have focused career goals and solid reasons for going back to school so soon after their undergraduate degree.

Similarly, older candidates will face challenges. Older candidates will have to prove that it makes sense to return to school at this late stage of their career, and that they are not merely encountering a mid-career crisis. They will also have to demonstrate that all of their time in the work world has been well spent. They should demonstrate progression, tangible contributions, and a high level of self-awareness, confidence, and maturity. A 37-year-old applicant who has spent 15 years in the same position without showing significant growth or progression will have a hard time being admitted to a top school. But this is not because they are 37 or because of the 15 years of experience. Rather, it is because they may have not demonstrated growth during that time. Any applicant who has choppy, inconsistent work experience or a stagnant career will benefit from the guidance provided in Chapter 35, where we discuss how to address these, and other, application challenges.

Young or old, if you can achieve all of the above, you can have a good shot at getting in to a program that is right for you, and should not be worried that you have hit some imaginary cut-off age. When deciding *if* you want to apply and where you want to apply, your age might be one element you consider, but it should *never* be the sole deciding factor.

Younger and older candidates

"I applied while still an undergraduate."

Daniel
HARVARD

When I said I wanted to apply to Stanford and Harvard as a senior in college (my college was not a highly ranked school), people thought I was crazy. Maybe I was crazy but I tend to be pretty focused on my goals. I would not have applied if I did not have a lot of work experience, but I did have a lot of part-time experience, starting from my sophomore year in college. When I read through the essay questions and saw what was asked of recommenders, I felt that I had great material to write about, even though my experience was all part time, during college. I had worked while studying abroad, during summers and part time at college during the normal school year. This was not just a job to make extra money, they were internship type positions that were related to my career goals and where I was able to get increasing levels of responsibility. I got a great rec from my boss. I also had a lot of involvements at school which I think really linked back to my leadership skills. I truly felt ready to apply. I know what I wanted to do and had been building on that for a few years, so even though I was young and "inexperienced," I had packed a lot into my years.

"I needed to be more focused than younger candidates"

Munish
U MICHIGAN, ROSS

I was four or five years older than the average candidate applying to the schools I was going for; it was an area of concern. As an older candidate, I decided I needed to have my career goals much more focused and streamlined; I didn't have the luxury of being even a little bit generic or dilly-dallying. Plus, I had five to six years of very applicable experience for the career I want to be in after my MBA. It turned out to be a strength.

"I had some issues with younger interviewers"

Edward
MIT, SLOAN

I was 30 when I applied. Being an older applicant had a few negatives. I had an interview with Chicago; the guy was two years out of undergrad and he's interviewing me. So, basically, I think the age thing was a factor for him. If you're an older candidate, I don't think you want to be interviewed by a current student, which means you probably don't want to set up an interview at the school. It's kind of weird being interviewed by a guy who is where you were four years ago.

I interviewed at Yale and was assigned a young interviewer from Europe. He had no idea what I was talking about. I had no idea what he was talking about. We didn't connect. It was a total mismatch. That's where this issue of luck in the application and interviewing process comes in.

If you're an older candidate, I don't advise you to visit the school for an interview. You may get one of the junior members of the admissions committee that has a chip on her shoulder and something to prove.

Once you're at business school, having the extra experience gives you a definite leg up…by far. So many of the younger students don't know what to focus on…in the classroom…in student life. Their priorities are a little screwed up. Some were really focused on getting all As, which is a little screwed up, because there weren't any levels of distinction at Sloan.

School Selection

CHAPTER 4

Developing Your List

Most applicants spend a great deal of time agonizing over their school list. This is viewed as a crucial first step that must be finalized before embarking on the process. Many applicants begin with a very long, ambitious list of schools and as they move forward some schools fall off, and others are added, for all kinds of reasons; the school list evolves, as does the applicant's story. Obviously, you need at least one school to start, but much of your list can be determined as you work through the process. As you become more invested in going to business school, and your story solidifies, you may decide to add additional schools. As you clarify your goals, you may consider schools that you had never looked at in the past. Similarly, this exercise may cause you to drop schools from your list.

As you form your list, one important question to ask yourself is: How committed am I to going to school *next year*? Am I dedicated to one or two top-choice schools, or to going back to school—period? Some applicants are content in their careers, and will only go back to school to attend a top choice. This is a fine decision—just realize that applying to one school is a risky strategy, no matter how qualified you may be. Other applicants put together a broader list in order to maximize chances of success. This is a personal decision—just be honest with yourself when assessing where you want to be next year.

It's also important to be aware of the different types of programs available. Depending on where you are in your life you may decide that a traditional 2-year, full-time program located across the country is just not an option. Fortunately, there are many alternatives, with more springing up regularly.

One-Year Programs—A number of excellent options exist for individuals who want to complete the MBA in only a year. These programs are accelerated versions of the two-year program and applicants should leave with the same set of knowledge and a similarly strong network. These programs are generally best for applicants with clear and consistent goals who are anxious to return to the work force quickly.

- A one-year program that runs 12 months, beginning in the summer, eliminates the possibility of a summer internship. Such programs generally require that applicants have completed undergraduate or graduate business courses in order to be eligible. This is an ideal program for those who already have a solid business base and are not seeking significant changes to their career path.
- An intermediate-length program, which may run for around 16 months. Such programs are geared to students who are returning to their prior job or a family

business, or who are planning to start their own business and thus do not require a summer internship.

- You can also find a school that offers only one-year programs, or, for example, an intensive, accelerated 10-month program, which may allow for a relatively brief internship.

Executive MBA (EMBA)—The Executive MBA is right for the more seasoned professional, who is already somewhat advanced in his or her career. A number of interesting programs target this population.

- Some schools have even joined together to offer programs such as bi-coastal MBA experiences for executives. Students in such programs typically are older and more experienced than those in a regular full-time program.
- Certain schools offer particularly innovative EMBA programs, in some cases ones that leverage Internet-enabled distance learning and incorporate international residencies in order to expose students to the international aspects of the current business world.

Part-Time or **FEMBA (Fully Employed MBA)**—The part-time MBA is ideal for the individual who wants to earn an MBA but cannot take time away from career. The part-time programs will enable you to balance school on a part-time basis with your full-time job. You graduate with the same degree and education, although frequently it takes a bit longer to get through the curriculum. Many part-time programs boast several locations in order to be most accessible to local working students.

- Many schools offer weekend and evening classes, often also leveraging the Internet to deliver course information efficiently to a busy professional. These

programs typically take two or three years to complete.

CHAPTER 5

Other Considerations

Putting together a school list is a very personal process. Although others can advise you with regards to "where you might be admitted," or "the school's reputation in X industry," in the end you need to make the call on where you will spend the next several months, and the name that will be on your resume for the rest of your life.

While I do encourage all applicants to be open-minded and thoroughly research a broad set of schools, I will never encourage you to apply to a school that you will not want to attend. It is always nice to have a wide range of options and apply to some schools that are not as competitive, but if you interact with a school and just know in your gut that you would not want to attend, why would you waste time and money applying?

In addition, if you have a dream school—that school that you have had your heart set on forever—you need to apply there! Even if others tell you that you have no chance, even if your stats are far below their reported numbers, if after doing your research you still really want to attend, you should apply. I would hate to see applicants go through a process successfully and end up at a great school, but always wonder "what if" about that top choice that they took off their list. While low numbers or less than stellar work experience can certainly limit your chances of being admitted, if you are truly a good fit for a school and can convey that in your application, you might be able to earn a spot in their class. And even if you are not admitted, at least you will have tried.

Many applicants have very specific career goals, right down to wanting to work in a certain capacity for a certain company. If you know where you want to work after graduation, you should call that company and find out what they think of a target school. I had a client who was based in NY and wanted to attend Columbia more than anything. She also had a short list of companies she was excited to target for her summer internship. I suggested she call one of her top companies to find out where they recruit. It turned out that they recruited on campus at only five schools, and Columbia was not one of them. They also told her that it was virtually impossible to secure an internship if you did not come from one of those five schools. This five-minute phone call significantly impacted her school list.

Finally, where you are in your life or career, and where you want to end up, can greatly influence your list of schools. Issues such as family or career satisfaction are important but often overlooked factors. If you realistically want to end up building your career in Los Angeles near your extended family, but are lured by the idea of an exciting two years in NY, you will have to weigh these considerations carefully as you make your decisions. Don't leave your family—especially a spouse or fiancé(e)—out of the mix in your decision-making process or you'll risk alienating your key "stakeholder" (trust me: you'll learn all about this kind of stakeholder analysis in b-school!).

One of the consultants that now works with Stacy Blackman Consulting applied to Haas and Harvard, and was admitted to both, when she went through her own process years ago. Many people are surprised to learn that she decided to attend Haas, which has a slightly lower ranking, because she was pursuing a career in the wine industry. Years after graduating, she is living in the Bay Area, pursuing the career of her dreams in the location of her choice, is closely aligned with Haas, and regularly leverages her network there. She absolutely has no regrets. In this case, she had to formulate her own personal rankings based on personal preference and a very focused career vision.

CHAPTER 6

Your "Window" for Applying: How Your Life and Career Impact the Choice and Number of Potential B-Schools

"How many schools should I apply to? Which schools should I apply to?"

These are key questions aspiring MBAs ponder during the spring and summer before the busy application-writing season in fall and winter. The answers are different depending on where the applicant is within his or her "window" of applying to business school. It's important to be aware of where you are in life and how this impacts your school decisions.

The vast majority of MBA students are in their mid-20s to early 30s. Only a small portion come directly from college and only a few attend full-time business school in their late 30s and into their 40s. But even within the, say, eight-year "window" from 24 to 32 years of age, applicants have a variety of inputs to consider when deciding the portfolio of MBA programs they should apply to.

Age: Many applicants in their mid-20s decide they will apply only to their first two choices this year, figuring they can reapply a couple years down the line when they have a bit more experience. I can understand this approach for some younger candidates, but applicants who are a bit older should strongly consider a different approach. They should apply to a wider array of schools to ensure that they will at least have the option of attending business school the next fall. Of course, the best scenario involves an intelligent mix of top schools and "safer" schools that will yield a choice of MBA programs for the applicant. Some candidates, frankly, get on an unreasoned "Harvard or Stanford...or nothing!" kick that doesn't serve anyone's interests.

Next career alternative: Some MBA aspirants are in positions in which they could continue on for many more years. Others hold roles at places like consulting firms or top investment banks where policy and/or tradition encourages young employees to acquire further education. In environments where one can continue to advance unfettered, a candidate might consider applying solely to his or her top-choice programs. However, candidates coming from companies with 2- to 3-year analyst programs that don't allow for much upward progression should probably cast their nets a bit wider, assembling a bigger portfolio of schools.

Career track satisfaction: I have talked to several MBA aspirants who feel they are "locked" in roles that are too technical or too narrowly defined. Yet, some still want apply to just a couple of very highly ranked programs. When people desire to make a career transition to an entirely new role or industry—sooner, rather than later—I highly encourage them to apply to a broader array of business schools. There are incredible programs throughout the top

20 in the b-school rankings (and even beyond) that can provide the classes, career programs, and alumni networks that aid this kind of transition.

First timer…or reapplicant?: A candidate who is going through his or her second round of business school applications should almost always apply to more schools. Candidates who are applying a couple of years down the line after dramatically improving their experience base might add a couple of new schools to the mix but still target their top programs from a few years before. However, candidates who are applying the very next year without significant changes in role, experience, or "extracurriculars" ought to pursue a different base of schools, with perhaps one or two holdovers from the year before.

Family considerations: Taking two years to get an MBA is not just a "business decision," it's a "life decision." Sometimes, the interests of boyfriends, girlfriends, husbands, wives, and children are critical factors in making the decision of if, when, and where to apply. These considerations are much more complex and varied than the factors listed above, so it's difficult to work through them in depth here. For instance, I knew some students who wanted to get through business school quickly so that they could start a family afterward, but I also knew of others who thought that business school (with day care, low travel requirements, flexible schedule, etc.) was a great environment in which to begin to build up their brood.

Candidates should talk with family, friends, and mentors (and potentially an MBA application advisor) early in the application process to determine where they are in this "window" for business school. It's an absolutely critical step in managing this multi-month application process thoughtfully.

CHAPTER 7

Research: Go to School on All Your Schools

Research is essential during this part of your process, as with the earlier process of deciding whether the MBA is right for you. By research we do not mean taking a quick look at the rankings and picking off the top few schools. We mean serious, first-hand research. You should note that if you do rely on rankings you could end up utterly confused, as the rankings can vary widely from school to school.

MBA Forums

There are often opportunities to attend larger events where many business schools come together to meet and greet prospective applicants. This is an opportunity to chat informally with representatives, gather brochures, and view a large number of schools at once. One example of a way to get great exposure to top schools is the MBA Tour, which hosts events in large cities around the world and has an impressive roster of programs in attendance. These forums can be a good first step to help you narrow down your list of schools. Following the larger forum, you may start to whittle down your list and focus more individually on specific target schools.

Information Sessions

If you cannot actually make it to campus, or even if you can, business school information sessions can be a great way to learn more about a particular program and interact with admissions representatives, students, or alumni. Information sessions are often held at local company headquarters or hotels in various cities. You can sign up online to receive information from a given school, and will then be notified about information sessions and various events, generally via email, throughout the application season. These sessions dominate the calendar in the late summer and early fall, and my clients always want to know whether these are worth attending. I believe they are.

Five good reasons to attend an information session:

1) The first rule of successful marketing is to know your target market. This means that up front you want to do a lot of research. Reading books, scouring the web, reviewing brochures—all of this is great. But nothing can replace actually meeting representatives from the schools and hearing first hand what makes their school special.

2) Building off of the point above, in addition to educating yourself, you may actually gather some great content for your essays and interview. You will inevitably be asked why you want to attend a certain school, and it is so much more powerful to speak

from first-hand experience rather than quoting the website.

3) The information you gather at these sessions may shatter stereotypes, helping you to refine your school list or consider a school you had not taken seriously in the past.

4) You may actually make a valuable contact. You could very well meet someone from the admissions committee, a current student or alum, and stay in touch. This could prove to be a valuable or enjoyable relationship down the road. As you draft your essays you may be able to contact this individual for an informational interview that could enrich the content of your essays.

5) It will help to immerse you in the process. Few things will motivate you to focus on your essays more than attending a session with 100 qualified competitors.

So, dress up in business attire, bring a list of questions and a handful of business cards, and head over to those information sessions. This is less about you making an impression than about the school making an impression on you. However, every impression counts and you certainly will want to be prepared! Read on for some information session "DON'Ts":

1) Don't ask questions for the sake of being noticed. If you have legitimate questions, go ahead and ask. This is the time to learn, so you are not expected to know everything about the school and to have already done your research. However, don't start asking questions just to make an impact and be seen.

2) Don't be overly aggressive with representatives and try to crowd out other applicants. Having served as

a representative for Kellogg at admissions events, I have cringed watching an aggressive prospect working hard to make a strong impression. Most schools are truly looking for collegial team players. Certainly, one way to make an impression is to elbow your way to the front of a pack of hungry applicants—but it will not be the type of impression you want to make.

3) Don't be sloppy. You don't necessarily have to wear your best suit, but clean and professional attire will help you fit in and feel perfectly comfortable.

4) Don't go with a bad attitude. If you are there, be there to learn. Try to keep an open mind, and truly learn about the school. If you learn that you do not want to apply there, that is fine. But you may be surprised and decide to apply to a school that was not on your list before. Feel free to take notes and accumulate insights that you can use in your essays.

The School Visit

I frequently am asked whether or not to visit target schools. A visit is certainly not necessary and most schools will tell you that it has no impact on their decision. However, if it is financially feasible and fits into your schedule, I always recommend a visit. The visit can help you decide where to apply. Walking across a campus, sitting in on a class, and interacting with students can greatly influence your decisions. This type of insight is incredibly valuable and should not be under-rated. Should you decide to apply to a particular school, there are other reasons why this visit will work to your benefit. When you visit the school, you develop a better understanding of the school's culture. This is sure to come through in your essays and interview. While others will be referencing the school website, you can cite specific first-hand experiences. When you visit, you will meet people and have specific experiences that you can highlight throughout your essays and interview. This adds color and individuality to your application.

Although schools understand that many people cannot make a visit, it definitely shows a strong interest in and commitment to a program when you make the effort to visit. This is particularly true if you are traveling a long distance. If you live nearby, not visiting is not an option!

If you do decide to visit, you should call the admissions office ahead of time and ask them about the following opportunities:

1) Can you sit in on a class?
2) Can you go on a tour of the school?
3) Are other types of information sessions available?
4) Can you interview on campus?

Thus, you are making it known that you are visiting and doing your best to take full advantage of this experience. Dropping in unexpectedly is discouraged because you will not be able to make the most of your visit.

If at all possible, you should make arrangements to stay with a current student. Perhaps you have a friend, or a friend of a friend who is a student. Doing this will allow you to see the more informal side of the school and help you to meet current students.

Enjoy yourself and be open minded. This is a fun opportunity to start planning a very exciting next step in your life.

Networking

Outside of formal school visits and information sessions, speaking with current students and alumni is helpful. These individuals will hopefully be very honest in sharing their experience with you. Even if they describe an aspect of the school that they love, it may not appeal to you. Some applicants are fortunate in that they are friends with or work with students and alums from every school. Others will need to be more creative. Perhaps you can network and speak with that friend of a friend. If not, call or email your target schools and ask to be connected with someone who may have similar interests. Or you can search online for contacts at relevant clubs and ask to speak with them. This will help to put you in touch with individuals who have similar academic interests and career goals.

Most schools will be able to accommodate this kind of request to help you do your research. When you have these conversations, make sure you have an agenda—know what you are looking for in a school and find out what your target schools have to offer. When it comes to informal networking, there are also some DON'Ts to consider:

1) Don't harass your contacts! Remember that they are taking time out of their extremely busy lives to help you. I have had clients excitedly forward me email correspondence that they have had with very accommodating contacts, and I cringe as I note the high volume of anxious and persistent email pings as the applicant works towards establishing a relationship. Be sure to limit your contact, and make sure each contact has a purpose other than rubbing shoulders with the individual.

2) Don't forget to say thank you. A show of appreciation can go a long way. If your contacts make time for you, be sure to show your appreciation.

3) Don't make contact without purpose. Have an agenda for your meeting or phone call, and stick to it. Your contact will expect you to have specific ques-

tions and will not necessarily appreciate an hour of chit-chat.

4) Don't leave them hanging. If contacts have made themselves available to you, it is always nice to follow up and inform them of your results at the end of your process. This relationship may be valuable or enjoyable later on so don't kill it just because you are finished with your application.

5) When you write your essays, don't just list a bunch of current students you spoke with at an information session—instead, illustrate the new information you learned from them.

Connecting with a school representative

"The personal connection"

Carl
UCLA, ANDERSON

One of the biggest risks I took in the process was when I met one of UCLA's admissions officers. It *had* been my plan to apply to the part-time program because I saw the test scores were lower and the admission percentages were more favorable. The most important thing was getting in somewhere and getting this MBA behind me.

I met an admissions officer who was a part of the full-time program and asked him who I should talk to about the part-time program. He asked why I wanted to apply to the part-time program and I gave him a very unvarnished answer. I told him that I had applied to the full-time program last time and been rejected and I had a level of urgency about getting into business school and getting on with my life, which I didn't see as being compatible with taking the risk of reapplying to the full-time program. He said, "Really?"—kind of shocked by my honesty. But then he said he thought the full-time program was better aligned with my goals. I told him, "Maybe you didn't hear what I said: you didn't let me in last time and I'm not taking that risk again." And he came back at me, "Maybe

you didn't hear me: I said you should apply to the full-time program…and I'm an admissions officer there." So, I applied, and was accepted.

"I had a very positive experience with an on-campus interview."

James
UNIVERSITY OF VIRGINIA, DARDEN

I was applying to US business schools from Europe and had several issues with my application. I had no activities outside of work, my numbers were below average and in general I did not understand the process well. I selected four schools to apply to and felt that Darden was my reach school. I had no intention of coming to the US to visit but finally decided to come to visit Darden when I was invited to interview because I wanted to learn more and hoped to show my interest in the program. When I was

there, it was clear to me that students and admissions people were extremely impressed that I had made the long trip. I had a great visit and learned a lot about the environment at the school and the attitudes of the students. I think that I performed quite well in my interview because I was enthusiastic from the experience. I ended up being admitted to Darden and not to any of the others, so have always felt that my visit was important to my success.

Planning Ahead and Improving Candidacy

We highly recommend beginning your application process early on, planning far in advance of deadlines. This does not mean that you will be drafting essays 12 months before they are due. It means that you will have time to actually focus on enhancing your candidacy *before* you start executing on the applications.

CHAPTER 8

Should You Have an Advisor?

Although we believe that it is best to have an advisor of some sort, it's certainly possible to do it all on your own. What follows, however, are our thoughts on what you should look for if you choose to have an advisor.

Your MBA application is a critical document that will have a major impact on the next several years of your life, your overall career trajectory, and your resume—forever. Just as authors have editors and athletes have coaches—and just as in life we seek advice from friends—in this incredibly important process, it may well be wise to ask for help. This is not a pitch to sell you on the type of comprehensive services offered by a consulting company. The MBA application process is very personal and there is probably no one company or resource that will be appropriate for everyone. However, as you plan for your MBA applications, you should consider what type of advice, guidance, and support you may wish to enlist.

Comprehensive Services

Comprehensive services are one of the key offerings of a large number of firms. This service covers many aspects of the process and essentially partners with you throughout the life of the process. For many people, it can be reassuring and extremely helpful to have that type of ongoing support. We certainly believe that there is a lot of value to be derived from this type of service, which can provide the intimacy of a one-to-one relationship with a dedicated consultant, along with the pooled knowledge base offered by an extended team and broader resources developed by an experienced company. Such resources may even include a forum through which clients share items such as successful essays and interview question lists, school overviews, and step-by-step guidance.

The perspective of consulting companies benefits from having seen many, many applications over many application cycles. After a while, advisors get a great feel for what works and what does not. Experienced counselors also know which types of stories are tired, and which might be more unique. Multiply this by an extended team and you have a pretty powerful resource.

This type of service will benefit someone who does not have a good feel for the multiple steps of the application process and who wants a resource that can help answer questions and navigate through some of the trickier issues. There are also applicants who have a lot of people around them to answer questions—folks working in a top consulting firm or investment bank are surrounded by MBA grads, for instance—but need more dedicated help positioning themselves and thinking through their personal approach. If an applicant wants more constant assistance, and plans to work through multiple drafts, purchasing a comprehensive package could be the way to go.

Hourly Services

Hourly services generally benefit an individual who has a better handle on the overall application but would like some help with specific, targeted aspects of the process. They feel confident managing their own process, and perhaps just want one hour here and two hours there to work through certain issues. These advisors are also often alums of top MBA programs who supplement their income by assisting clients on a short-term basis. Many larger consulting companies offer this, as do independent consultants who have some familiarity with the process and charge by the hour for their help.

Editor

Many applicants feel extremely comfortable with the MBA application process and with their own strategy but are not comfortable with their writing skills. They are concerned with the best way to articulate their ideas in writing and want someone to help smooth out their language. An editor might not need to know anything about MBA admissions—but he or she needs to know how to write. If you are looking for help in this area of your application, you can likely save some money and hire a strong writer or editor to provide feedback on your written materials. You can even use online resources like Craigslist to find an accomplished editor who has worked with applicants for colleges and graduate schools.

Friends and Family

Many applicants have friends, family members, and/or co-workers who can help in these areas. You may have a brother who is a great writer, a cousin who graduated from Harvard, or a friend who served on an admissions committee. Indeed, these individuals may possess some of the same skills as people that you would hire. Your consultants/editors/advisors are only human at the end of the day, and there are other individuals who can provide you with advice. Similarly, the advice you get from a consultant can be replicated by a smart friend who understands your industry! If you feel that you have a team at your disposal that will help you out for free, you may indeed be able to manage your own process without hiring an outside resource.

If you do decide to go it alone and depend on personal support, make sure that your "team" is willing to put in the time to thoughtfully review your work and provide feedback in a timely manner. Chapter 44, "Too Many Cooks in the Kitchen," provides some guidelines for lining up personal contacts to review your work. Keep in mind that you are looking for thoughtful, informed feedback from a small group of people who are truly willing to invest the time on your behalf.

Managing Your Help

As with any management relationship, you need to know how to manage effectively in order to maximize results. Remember that if you are working with outside resources, you will need to factor in time for their review when you are putting together a timeline. Cramming an entire application into one week may work for your "operate best under pressure" approach, but it certainly does not leave much time for thoughtful feedback and multiple iterations. Working

with an advisor of any kind should make the overall process more efficient, effective, and successful, but it can
slow down the time between each step as there is some
back and forth. You will also want to make sure that each
helper is clear on his or her role. For example, Mom and
Dad might know nothing about MBA applications, but they
know you well. So you may very well ask them their opinion
on whether the essence of you comes out. The friend of
a friend who served on an admissions committee and
offered to look at your essays should be providing insight
into whether you have effectively positioned yourself for a
particular school. The editor that you hire who knows little
about applications can provide guidance on grammar, style
and tone, but not content.

No outside individual should be offering to write an
application for you. Clearly this is unethical and just not
allowed by business schools. Even beyond ethics, it is an
unwise strategy for someone who is serious about being
admitted to a top-choice school. Ultimately, *you* are the
best person to be explaining your character and all of your
unique points. Your voice, philosophy, and sense of humor
should appear consistent throughout the application and in
your interview. While hiring a ghostwriter may be tempting
in the short term, it is highly unlikely to lead to longer term
success. Whoever is writing your application is likely writing
many others and you will all sound the same. Admissions
committees tend to be pretty good at sniffing out these
types of situations. So, by not doing the work yourself, you
will be hindering your chances on many fronts.

This isn't the time for shortcuts. You may find that a
good advisor is actually making you work harder! He or
she might tell you your app can be improved upon when
you thought you were finished. And he or she may ask you

probing questions to help you think through new ideas or take a different approach.

Overall, it is often wise to enlist some additional eyes to look at your applications. When we re-read our own writing, we see what we know we intended to write, not necessarily what is actually on the printed page. Whether you hire a company or individual or enlist your own team of supporters will depend on your distinct needs and style, but it is not advisable to submit this all-important document without someone to provide a reality check.

Do you need advice from an outsider?

Sashi
UNIVERSITY OF VICTORIA, BC

I started the process on my own for the first-round schools. I found I was very frustrated going through the application process on my own and only having one set of trusted eyes to look over everything. I wasn't sure what I should portray myself as and my motivation level was falling…I would keep putting off my work. I wasn't even confident if I was a good MBA candidate. When I started working with an admissions consultant I understood more and more about what the business schools were looking for and how I should portray myself. Having someone experienced just gave me a direction to follow.

Omar
CORNELL

The best advice I got about essays from my admissions consultant was "Tell a story, don't just say it." You have to give real examples. Don't just say what you did, tell them how you did it. Instead of claiming "I'm a motivated person," show lots of examples where you did this thing and that thing when you really didn't have to.

One of the most helpful exercises you can do

to prepare for applying is just to fill out a "Brag Sheet" with your achievement and experiences in work, school, and extracurriculars. You should include special interests or hobbies. Just get it all out there to get new ideas of where to draw content from. Then you can discuss all of these things with a professional advisor, MBA alums or trusted friends. I had done extra research with professors during my undergrad days, and I didn't know that it would be valued at a graduate level. Most likely I would have overlooked that if I hadn't written it down and then talked about it with my advisor.

Edward
MIT SLOAN

The questions are so broad and so open-ended. There's a big benefit to brainstorming for a while to find essay ideas the committee will find appealing. That's the hardest thing to do. It's a real benefit to working with an advisor. Doing that kind of brainstorming and idea generation on my own would have been

the biggest challenge. You need someone who's been through it to say, "That idea sucks. This one sounds good." In my first attempt applying to schools, I didn't get any interviews. My second time around, working with an advisor, I got into a bunch. It wasn't like I had changed that much as a person, my applications just put me in a much stronger light.

Munish
UNIVERSITY OF MICHIGAN, ROSS

If you choose to get outside help, I think selecting the right admissions consultant is really, really important. If you start off on the wrong foot, you may be heading down a path which can never play out well for you. I started working with a consultant to whom I would send my essays three to four days in advance of a call. Then I would get a call from her saying, "Let's just postpone the call half an hour." She would read the material I had sent three days earlier just five minutes before talking to me, and I thought I was getting the short end of the stick. She should have been prepared to speak with me immediately and that was never the case.

More frequent interactions with an admissions consultant can give you a lot of new ideas about which experiences to write about and how to position them. If you have infrequent interactions or just communicate with e-mail, something is lacking big time. They are just an editor, then. I worked with that original advisor for a month and never got a sense of any major philosophy or approach she had. Then I moved on to another advisor.

In the beginning, I had not even thought about showing my emotions in any of my essays. But after consultations with my admissions consultant and seeing the outcome of how the first essays were shaping up, I got more comfortable with it. In Wharton's outsider essay, I wrote about the very emotional experience of being the only sighted person in a conference filled with blind people. Once I got into the rhythm of it, and once I came to terms with showing my human or softer side, the essays flowed really well. They were nailed down after only a couple of edits.

TALES FROM THE ROAD

All the advice I received from the second consultant while preparing my application was invaluable. If I had to pick one single piece of advice, it would be to personalize my essays to the point that no single sentence in it could have been written by any other person. Anyone could write "I'll learn how to create product marketing strategies from the Marketing class." I should focus on my unique learning/take-away from that class for my future goals.

CHAPTER 9

Don't Lose that Great Idea: Keep a Notebook During Spring and Summer

Jack Kerouac kept a notebook before he went O*n the Road*. Larry David's notebook of wry observations and embryonic comedy routines was lost and then found by annoying fans on "Curb Your Enthusiasm." Now, *your* notebook should play a big part of your business school admissions process.

During spring and summer, commit to carrying around a notebook to scratch down your thoughts about your applications. Some of these might be random ideas that come to you while you're working at your desk, sitting on a plane, or braving the morning commute (if you drive, however, please keep two hands on the wheel at all times). But you should also plan to spend, say, half an hour of scheduled quality time per week with your notebook for several months. You may choose to use your notebook computer as your notebook in order to more easily reformat your thoughts into essay outlines.

If you are starting to think about applications before most essay questions have been published, know that most of the themes are universal from year to year and should not come as a surprise to applicants. If you are not familiar with the basics of essay questions, go online and look at the prior year's applications for a few schools. You will probably notice some common themes. Take time to write down your preliminary ideas relating to:

1) Your main career accomplishments to date: not responsibilities or your job description, but your achievements

2) Examples of your leadership abilities

3) Outside interests and passions and main achievements you've had in your "extracurricular" life

4) People and events that have influenced you

5) Your career goals after business school…and your broader life goals

6) Areas in which you need improvement or personal development: these may be demonstrated skill or personality weaknesses you've committed to improve upon. Also, these may be areas you have just not had a chance to develop yet.

7) How business school will benefit you: everyone benefits from "the diverse student body, world-renowned faculty, and active alumni network"; you need to move well beyond this level of analysis. What specific things do you want to learn? What classes do you want to take? What would be your ideal summer internship?

Don't settle for writing down your general thoughts. Be specific. As a matter of fact, be incredibly specific. I encourage my clients to employ what I call "micro-examples" to bring their essays to life. That means finding those discrete moments that encapsulate major experiences in your life. That one negotiation session where your idea led to a breakthrough…the discomfort of the first time you had to fire someone…that phone call where you lost an important customer's business…the "ah-hah" moment when you decided to invest in a certain entrepreneur's company.

Some other things to scratch on your pad:

1) Your thoughts on what schools are right for you. What departments need to be great? What geography do you prefer? Are programs such as cross-registration important for you?

2) Who will your best recommenders be—and what do you want them to say?

3) Comments from your friends and family, and colleagues if appropriate. Your business school application process can be a great time to buff up your ego. Sit down with your buddies and ask them: "What are the best things about me?" Sometimes outside perspectives will reveal things about your character and talents that you weren't fully aware of. Actually, in addition to buffing up your ego, you should probably also ask these people about their feelings on those areas of personal and professional development that you should be working on.

Your notes will be an incredibly valuable resource, whether you're tackling the admissions process by yourself or working with an applications advisor.

CHAPTER 10

Interesting Books for Aspiring MBAs (don't worry: no GMAT prep manuals here)

Setting aside time to read over the months before diving into your applications is one of the smartest things you can do to enhance your candidacy for top-flight MBA programs. Many candidates have not read a book for personal enjoyment or education for years, and they often don't consider the busy summer and fall before MBA application season a good time to start up again. But when you examine the list of reasons for diving into some good books over the next several months, it really seems like a no-brainer. Reading can:

- Improve your vocabulary and mastery of grammar: reading is a change of pace from GMAT prep, but can still help you in this area.
- Improve your writing: your b-school essays will represent one of the biggest and most important writing projects of your life. Getting ideas about interesting

sentence structures and storytelling methods will be invaluable.

- Give you more to write about: you may think of whole new essay ideas or refine ideas about certain sections of essays.
- Give you more to talk about: business school interviewers want to learn about the "full you." Many interviews go into current events, history, politics, etc., so if you can demonstrate that you've kept aware of the world outside of your cubicle, you're a step ahead of the game.

Demonstrate Your Passions

By no means is it necessary to plow through a stack of the latest business books so that you can drop buzzword after buzzword in your essays and interviews. And you shouldn't feel obligated to round out the "weak" areas of your business experience by hitting the local bookstore to get *Stocktrading for Dummies* or *Marketing for Dummies.* After all, we go to business school in order to learn about disciplines that are new to us.

The most important thing is to further develop your own interests and passions, not demonstrate that you are a member of the "Warren Buffett Book of the Month Club." If you are interested in art, read about that. If you are intrigued by the history of baseball, immerse yourself in it. If medical science advances fascinate you, find some gems in this arena. Of course, it never hurts to develop some form of "business perspective" on the subjects you feel passionately about. For instance, if you love reading about medicine, mix in some books about, say, the economics of the healthcare system in the United States or the behavior of the global pharma industry.

If you wish to transition to a new sort of career after business school, demonstrating this kind of commitment can be particularly important. If you have been an IT consultant for the last five years, but want to become an entrepreneur and launch a new restaurant concept, you should show a commitment to the area that goes beyond spending your $50 consulting per diem in the finest restaurants your client's city has to offer. Reading about consumer trends, restaurant/retail entrepreneurs, or the organic food movement helps show that you follow your interests, you don't just talk about them.

My personal recommendation list includes works ranging from Thomas Kuhn's *The Structure of Scientific Revolutions*—which essentially introduced the term "paradigm shift" into the study of many subjects, including business—to Nick Hornby's *Songbook*—an excellent book of reasonably short essays that will entertain you while you absorb ideas on how to structure your own short-form essays. Please see our website www.mbaroadmap.com for the full list.

To reiterate: read anything, just read! That's the key element—thinking about words, structures, ideas, and storytelling, and exposing yourself to something new.

CHAPTER 11

Improve Your Candidacy, Then Improve Your Application (or What You *Should* Do on Your "Summer Vacation")

For people applying to major business schools, October, November, and December will inevitably be months filled with typing, spell-checking, typing, editing, typing, proofreading…and then some more typing. Choosing which bullet format looks best on the resume. Finding synonyms for all of the words one overuses. Spending two hours cutting the final 50 words from a 500-word essay. Incredibly fun stuff.

But May, June, July, and August can be very fruitful months both for your personal development and for improving your business school application—or, more precisely, for improving your business school candidacy.

Many b-school aspirants see the spring and summer solely as a time to take a GMAT prep course. They often wait until they are neck deep in the process of writing their essays and compiling all of their other application materials to identify the elements of their candidacy they wish to improve. Or, I should say, the elements they wish they had improved when they had the time. But, with a little advanced planning and a commitment of just a few hours a week, applicants can do a great deal to bolster their overall candidacy before that final rush of the fall and winter.

Seek Out New Responsibilities at Work

Applicants who take stock of their professional accomplishments in the months ahead of their application process may just end up seeing some holes. Scratch that: they will *always* see holes. Filling holes is what getting an MBA is all about. But we want to make sure we have demonstrated some skill and capability for growth in the areas we have targeted for our future careers. Sometimes, it makes sense to make progress in these areas before business school. Even just a couple of assignments in a new area can confirm that you are indeed interested and that you have the capacity to achieve at a high level in the future.

For instance, I once mentored an MBA applicant who had spent several years in the technology field working as an engineer on advanced microelectronics. Basically, he was working with wires and chips all day. We had started our dialogue over six months before his first MBA applications were due and we came up with a plan to improve his *managerial cred*. He committed himself to augmenting his case that he could be a great leader at a high-technology company in the future. The next Monday after our conversation he talked to his managers about taking on responsibilities that would let him develop as a business leader. They responded to his initiative by assigning him to be the liaison between his group and other departments within the company. The new role emphasized communication, negotiation, and project management, and required a keen understanding of organizational behavior. His overall career was probably helped out by this move, and his candidacy and b-school apps definitely were.

Travel

You've worked hard the last several years. You're going to spend a ton of hours cooped up studying for that pesky GMAT. And in the fall you're going to spend 50 to 100 hours in front of your computer writing and editing essays.

You deserve a vacation.

But instead of just making a quick jaunt to Vegas for golf and gambling or a "shop 'til you drop" trek to Manhattan, consider planning a vacation with a dual agenda of fun and personal enrichment. Injecting a bit of a learning agenda into your trip can expand your personal horizons, help more fully define your career objectives, and provide you more material for essays and interviews.

One candidate I've worked with was considering taking a vacation to Florida; instead, he traveled to a different tropical locale where he could both enjoy some quality beach time and participate in an environmental restoration program.

If you're interested in a career in technology after business school, but don't have much experience in the area, consider traveling to the Bay Area, attending some tech events, and setting up some networking time with entrepreneurs. You'll still be able to kite surf on the Bay and enjoy a day in the Napa Valley.

If you're interested in international business but haven't really gained much exposure to foreign cultures since your Eurail pass expired in 2002, plan a holiday to an interesting overseas locale. While there, see if you can pick out a few things in the local economy that seem different in your home economy: the products people buy, the brands they love, the kinds of technology they favor, the level of service you experience, etc.…

Community Service/Extracurricular Activities

Business schools pride themselves in training future leaders, not just educating a bunch of people who know how to calculate an IRR and overuse the word "leverage." They look for individuals who are concerned about doing great work and improving the world around them. Some young business people feel that even though they have not prioritized "extracurricular" activities early in their careers, they will definitely emphasize these sorts of activities once they are more established. However, more often than not, the patterns we establish toward community activities early in our careers remain fairly steady. If you feel that your commitment over the last several years to outside causes does not reflect the balance you want to establish in your life…well, put your money where your mouth is and get involved.

If you haven't been participating in outside activities, look up a few opportunities on the internet and get involved next weekend. It's really as simple as that, to be honest. Candidates who get involved even early in the year they apply will have a six- or even nine-month track record by the time apps are due. True, young professionals work long hours and often have demanding travel schedules, sometimes ruling out activities such as Big Brothers/Sisters or tutoring. But the next person I meet who cannot take out two hours on a weekend to help clean up a park or paint a school or talk with seniors at a nursing home will be the first.

If you have been involved with outside activities over

the last couple of years, consider stepping your activities up a notch. As detailed in a Tale from the Road following this chapter, one of my clients had helped out for a few hours a month for two years at a local Ronald McDonald House. In the fall, he ratcheted up his involvement by organizing some fundraising/recruiting events for young professionals.

To some, ramping up involvement in community activities may seem like "gaming the system." I personally don't feel this way at all. The community benefits by getting extra labor, at the very least, and maybe even the talents and creativity of a gifted individual. You benefit by deepening your involvement in causes that are meaningful to you. If the side effect of this is that your candidacy for b-school is in some way enhanced, all the better.

Leverage Your Interests

Why are extracurricular activities important to begin with?

1) They show that an individual is multi-dimensional. They demonstrate interests, passions, and personality. As such, they help the admissions committees get to know you beyond your professional goals.

2) Being involved outside of work shows that you can balance multiple commitments, and that you are the type of person who will be able to balance academics with clubs, conferences, recruiting, and more, once you are at school.

3) They can show that you have a larger view of the world—that you see what is happening outside of your office and you are interested in being involved and contributing in some way. They can show that

you understand your own role as a leader and your ability to leverage your position and give back.

4) They make you a more interesting person—someone that can contribute to the diversity and vitality of a class and alumni network.

5) It's an opportunity to demonstrate qualities such as creativity, leadership, teamwork, communication skills, and initiative. These qualities are important outside of a professional setting as well as at work.

Unfortunately, if you have spent the past five years buried in your office, "joining" an organization at the very last minute or volunteering at a soup kitchen one Sunday is not going to help you much. That kind of effort is pretty transparent. The schools realize that many of you are extremely busy with demanding jobs and committing to several hours a week is not possible. Still, the most successful applicants find ways to carve out time for interests and contributions.

When thinking about ways to become involved, don't get hung up on traditional volunteer work. There are many, many ways to become involved and highlight your unique contributions. A good place to start is with your own interests and passions. Think hard about what excites you, and how you can leverage those interests. A couple of examples from my clients:

Client 1: Enjoyed painting as a hobby until she accepted an investment banking job out of college. She felt she had no time to become involved outside of work. She rekindled her interest in art when she became involved in a company-sponsored fundraising initiative. She designed t-shirts to raise extra money and unite the team.

Result: Showcased her artistic talent and interest,

became involved in a great cause, and demonstrated creativity and leadership.

Client 2: Was on the swim team throughout high school and college. She decided to mentor through coaching a middle school swim team. Consequently, she developed meaningful relationships with the kids on her team and ended up learning a great deal from them.

Result: Showcased athletic interests and found a personally meaningful way to give back to her community. Highlighted important coaching and motivational skills.

Client 3: Struggled with learning English in Israel. Started an English Public Speaking Club in Israel and grew it over the course of four years.

Result: Highlighted a creative approach to solving a personal problem. Came up with a solution that helped others as well. Demonstrated leadership and ability to get things done.

You can see that Habitat for Humanity is not always the answer. Keep in mind that quality is far more important than quantity. Rattling off a list of 10 involvements will not help as much as something that truly reflects who you are and can showcase important interests and skills. You may be surprised to find that these involvements will add a great deal to your life, which is exactly the point!

Showing you have multiple dimensions to your experiences

"I had no extracurricular activities."

Jamie
KELLOGG

I started planning my MBA strategy many months in advance of deadlines. My strength was that I did have some very interesting work experience. I had worked for a small start-up in the education space as one of the first employees and it had grown and done very well.

The job had been all consuming and I had zero experience to speak to outside of work. However, I had some great ideas for non-profits linked to my work in education and decided to put some wheels into motion during the six-month period prior to

deadlines. My ideas linked into my career goals as well and just tied up the application very nicely. It was not that hard to come up with some ideas—the tough part was executing and I really wanted to show milestones in my application so that I did not just write "I have an idea!" I wrote a business plan, recruited a partner, and then went and pitched our program to some schools that I already had contacts in. We piloted the program for free and then started to try to spread out to other schools. I did worry that my timing would appear suspicious—why did I just start my organization right before business school?—and also, it was not like I had even a year of results to speak to. But I feel strongly that despite the youth of my non-profit and the timing, it did add to my application. It just gave me more content for certain essays and really added depth to my career goals story. Without the work experience I had, I do not believe I could have gotten this thing off the ground at all, so I also feel that it highlighted skills, experience and contacts that I had developed through work. Overall, very happy that I did this and feel it made my application a *lot* stronger.

"Upping my involvement"

Edward
MIT SLOAN

When they ask about activities you do, you don't just want to say "I've volunteered once or twice." You need to have one or two strong things that really stand out that you can talk about in depth. I had been involved with the Ronald McDonald House, but in the six months before my applications were due, I really upped my involvement. I organized a fundraiser at my house and a number of other activities.

CHAPTER 12

Other Candidacy Issues: Consider This Before You Tackle Your Applications

Transcript

Many applicants have a selective memory when it comes to their transcript. They remember the 3.8 in their psychology major but have somehow blocked out the C in Calculus and the overall 2.7. Your transcript is what it is, and it will not change, no matter how many classes you take after the fact. However, if you have low grades, there are things you can do to somewhat offset the damage. Get your hands on a copy of your transcript in advance of applying and carefully look at your performance. The following are some potential transcript issues that you can tackle head on with a bit of advance planning:

- Low overall GPA—A low overall GPA may raise a red flag for an admissions committee. They are seeking individuals with a track record of excellence, who prioritize academics and achievement, and who have the ability to excel academically. By taking a few classes now, you can help to offset some of their concerns. While straight A's in post-undergraduate courses will not erase your original transcript, you can demonstrate that you have the ability to excel academically, that you have identified a weakness and are making an effort to rectify it, that you are committed to learning, and that you can balance multiple commitments successfully. All of this can help mitigate the damage done by poor undergraduate performance. In addition, part of their concern is not linked to your academic abilities, but to your commitment to academics, your drive, and your ability to handle a full schedule. In essence, the "softer" aspects behind a high or low GPA. Later on, in your essays, you may have an opportunity to address these issues.

- Low grades in business or quantitative classes— Even if your overall GPA is high, if the two classes that you bombed were Calculus and Statistics, this could raise concerns about your ability to excel in a rigorous business school curriculum. For some of the same reasons as detailed above, taking relevant classes now will help to put the admissions committee at ease. You can retake the same classes that you struggled with as an undergrad, or you can take similar, business and quant-focused classes. Certainly, nailing the quant portion of the GMAT will also help to mitigate their worries in this area.

- No business or quantitative courses on the transcript—If you are currently in a business role that does not require fluency with business or numbers, and you do not have any of these types of courses on your transcript, you might consider taking a class now. This will demonstrate an awareness of your deficiencies and help to provide a level of comfort around your abilities. It will also show that you are aware of and committed to addressing any deficiencies in your background.

When you sign up for classes, don't worry too much about the prestige of the school. Business schools understand that you may not have a world class university nearby, and need a convenient option. So you should worry less about the school, and more about the coursework. If you happen to sign up too late to actually report your grades when you apply, letting the admissions committee know that you are currently taking a class (or classes) counts as well. And many schools will be open to hearing from you once you do receive your grades, even if your application has already been submitted. Finally, suggested courses to take are Calculus, Statistics, and Accounting. These basics will set the groundwork for a typical MBA curriculum.

Recommenders

Many applicants have obvious options for their recommenders. Others find selecting recommenders to be a more stressful event. If you do not have an obvious choice, you might want to use the months prior to the application to think about who will be a good fit for this role and to work on cultivating a stronger relationship. Establish these individuals as mentors, discuss your business school plans with them, and, in general, increase frequency of contact. Feel them out to determine who will be an appropriate choice so that you are not left scrambling at the last minute.

GMAT

Plan to take the GMAT during this candidacy stage, prior to applications being published, which usually happens over the summer. For *most* programs, the first half of the calendar year is a good time to focus on candidacy, including GMAT. Once you see the amount of work that goes into your essays and general application you will be thrilled to have the exam out of the way.

CHAPTER 13

GMAT Plan: Scheduling, Studying, Scoring

As we outlined above, the months before the actual application crunch period are a good time for your GMAT. Don't think of the GMAT as a one-day exam. Like other aspects of the application, the GMAT is a process and you must plan ahead.

It's important to understand how most of the top schools review your GMAT score. By and large, the GMAT score is self-reported on your application. This means that the school will ask you for your highest score, or perhaps your highest and most recent, and you manually input the information into your data forms. This self-reported score is really the only one that the admissions committee will look at until you are admitted. Once you are admitted, they will confirm the validity of the self-reported scores with the official GMAT score report. As a result, your highest score really, truly, is the one that is considered. I have been asked many times, and in turn have asked the schools—"Do you really consider the highest score?" The answer always comes back as a "yes."

Does this mean that you should keep taking the test as much as possible until you see improvement? Absolutely not. You have much better things to do with your time and money. However, I do recommend planning to take the test at least twice. There is no harm in taking it twice, and because this test becomes easier with practice, there is a good chance that you will improve your score. Beyond two attempts it is really up to you—if you feel that you have a reasonably strong chance of significant improvement, you may decide to continue to divert time away from other activities and give the test another try.

What if you take the test and know, without a doubt, that you completely bombed it? Should you cancel your score? Again, since the admissions committee considers your highest score, there is no point in canceling a low score. Every year I have clients who are convinced they floundered and were very pleasantly surprised. Those who cancel their scores are at a disadvantage—they have no idea how they scored, they are unable to "anchor," and thus there is no way of measuring improvement. Even if you do score low, it is nice to know where you stand, so that you can intelligently plan your next steps.

What is the score that you should be shooting for? The obvious answer is that you go for your highest possible score. Even if you received a 710 on your first attempt, a 760 is significantly better. If you are truly confident that you can improve that much, it is worth trying. That said, most of us cannot reach 760. The minimum you should shoot for is the range that encompasses the middle 80% of the class for your target school. Within that range—again, the higher the better. For example, if 80% of the class scored between

650 and 740, you would definitely want to strive to at least hit 650. Know that certain demographic profiles can get away with lower scores. It is true that a French female applicant, for whom English is a second language, may not be required to have as high a score as a Caucasian male from the US. If you are unable to reach the bar that you set for yourself, take comfort in the fact that 10% of students fall below that 80% mid-range. The rest of your application will have to work that much harder for you, but it is not impossible to overcome a low score.

Finally—preparation. While everyone has his or her own style and approach for preparing for the GMAT, I recommend a formal class or private tutor of some kind. Beyond the curriculum, a key benefit of a class is the discipline it provides. Between classes, homework, and practice tests, you are likely to make the GMAT a part of your daily routine and gain the practice that you need. Because the test is taken on a computer in a strange environment, practice and familiarity with the test is crucial. You should allow about two months for prep, and ideally you will not be distracted by essays and other aspects of the process during that time. All in all, two to three months is a fair amount of time to budget for the GMAT, when you consider study, first attempt, and then possible restudy and retake. Having that out of the way when you work on the application is a big bonus, so try to schedule all of this during the first half of the calendar year, during your "candidacy" phase.

Your Application
Timeline/Preparation

CHAPTER 14

Time Management: Prepare Your Calendar NOW for Your MBA Application Process

"**Time is on our** side." So quoth the Rolling Stones. Truer words were never spoken about the business school application process. Smartly investing and budgeting time is a key to generating the great essays needed to accurately represent your achievements, talents, goals, and potential contributions to a top b-school admissions committee. But, if you neglect tending to your calendar and work schedule, then time will most decidedly not be on your side.

Candidates need to balance the significant investment of hours spent developing essays with the other commitments in their lives: work, family, community service, friends, etc. The best way to do this is to start to put together your application calendar and time budget months before the deadlines you are targeting. Candidates need to think about time management from a number of angles.

Finding the HOURS: Enough Time to Grind Out Those Essays

Although the time MBA aspirants take to generate their applications varies greatly depending on writing ability, general work efficiency, and other factors, you should basically plan on spending 40 to 60 hours in front of your computer working on your collection of, say, four to eight applications. This amount of time generally covers the writing, revising, editing, proofing, formatting, and inputting of essays. Someone currently immersed in writing and editing as a part of his or her career—maybe someone authoring investment reports or working in corporate communications—will probably have a much smoother process than a person who has been imprisoned in Excel Hell for the last three or four years. Non-native English speakers will also probably need to plan on spending more time on their applications.

Aside from the essays themselves, candidates need to set aside the hours necessary to prep recommenders and continue with the reading, community service, and other activities that enhance their candidacy. Oh…and of course, we can't forget the hours of fun and frolic spent prepping for the GMAT.

Planning the DAYS: The Best Ways to Structure Your Work Sessions

Different folks have different sorts of work patterns. Some are most efficient when they can break up tasks into manageable pieces. Some work best when they can devote eight hours at a time in marathon writing sessions. MBA applicants should be aware of the way they work the most effectively and efficiently and structure their writing/editing sessions accordingly.

I recommend to most of my clients that they allocate two to three hours each time they sit down at their computer to work on their essays. Shorter sessions, I believe, don't allow enough time for people to get into a "literary groove." Essays should be handled holistically, especially in the first two drafts. Don't think that you're going to have a strong end-product if you steal 15 minutes here and 30 minutes there to generate that Wharton leadership answer. Essays composed in pieces often read as disjointed, unpolished tracts.

Most applicants should also avoid the "marathon session." It is the rare individual who is as sharp or creative eight hours into a writing and editing session as he was at the beginning. If you need to catch up by doing extra work, try breaking it up with a session in the morning and another in the evening.

Budgeting the WEEKS: Allow Enough Time for Reflection and Feedback

While some people think they produce their best work under intense pressure, it is extremely unwise to try to polish off a set of applications in just a week or two. Distributing the work over a sensible time period of four to six weeks lets you maintain a steady, but manageable pace. Spreading the work out a bit allows you to reflect on material you may have written over previous days; you may think of a better micro-example to illustrate a certain character trait or develop much more interesting or humorous language for a specific paragraph. This will not happen if you are forced to work at warp speed.

Distributing your writing and editing over a reasonable period also makes it easier for friends, family, or colleagues to provide feedback on your essays if you choose to ask them. It's extremely unfair to ask someone to turn around comments in a 24-hour period, so provide them a few days to give you their comments and critiques. And of course, leave yourself adequate time to reflect on and incorporate their feedback. Don't be one of those applicants who sends essays out to a friend in the last couple of days just for the sake of gaining the "security blanket" that comes with hearing "Great job! I know you'll get in." Select people who will tell you the real deal and give yourself enough time to act on it.

Finally, if you choose to work with a professional application advisor, make sure you take this into account in your calendar. Advisors in some ways make the process take longer—with the extra discussions and feedback cycles—but can also save time when all is said and done by helping make sure you don't follow any "dead ends" in your essay writing process.

Approach, process and timelines

"Invest the extra hours"

Carl
UCLA, ANDERSON

When it comes to the GMAT, I figured I was never going to be smarter mathematically than when I just got out of college…but that turned out to not be true. The second time I took it, I practiced quite a bit and was able to impact the score quite substantially.

I spent 30-40 hours researching, deciding which schools I wanted to apply to and attending MBA fairs. The writing of the essays, which is something I'm not naturally very good at—plus, I was a reapplicant and wanted to spend extra time on that part—I would figure it took me at least 80 hours to get through that part.

The biggest mistake I made first time was applying late. I think it's of critical importance to get the application in during the first round. Maybe the second round. From the second time when I applied, my biggest mistake was not applying to more "stretch" schools. From how I performed at Anderson, I think I would have performed pretty darn well at any of the top tier schools. So, maybe it was a mistake to not apply to more of the top schools. But, based on the fit and the "vibe" I got from Anderson, I might have gone there anyway.

"More schools, more choices"

Edward
MIT, SLOAN

The process took about six months. I would tell people to focus on the essays and worry less about visiting the schools. You have to focus your essays and really package yourself up as someone they are looking for. For almost the entire time, I was working most weekends and some of the evenings as well.

Apply to more schools, rather than fewer. There's quite a bit of luck to it, so you gotta go for some numbers and get some more applications in. Apply to 10 schools just to be more safe and to have more options. The amount you spend on applying to the extra schools is minimal when you compare to your total investment, including time.

CHAPTER 15

Which Round?

Rounds

Planning your application schedule obviously requires that you know your deadlines. Schools will generally announce their deadlines over the summer months. While every school is different, most schools have a number of deadlines, known as "rounds." Deciding in which round to apply can certainly complicate your planning. Frequently, the first deadline, round 1, will take place in the Fall, the second deadline, round 2, in the Winter, and the third deadline, round 3, in Spring. For each round there is a full admissions cycle and a unique set of notification dates. There are exceptions to this all over the place with some schools having fewer or more rounds and many variations on dates. That said, when faced with several different options, applicants want to know: "which round is the best round in which to apply?"

For many, there is a frenzy involved with trying to submit

applications in round 1. So much so that you might wonder what the other rounds are for. If everyone needs to submit applications in round 1, who exactly is being admitted in round 2? The answer: a lot of people are admitted in round 2, and if your application is not ready, you should not be afraid to slide to round 2.

All things being equal, round 1 may be a bit of a smarter strategy. At the beginning of round 1, all of the seats in the class are available. At the beginning of round 2, a bunch of seats have already been given away, and you are also competing with those on the waitlist. But then of course, there are those who say that all of the top candidates are applying in round 1—and you are up against the toughest competition. So then, maybe it is best to apply in round 2. Hmmm…this is confusing…

The truth is that the admissions committees know what they are looking for. They have become pretty good at estimating numbers, and evaluating and accepting applicants that fit their criteria. The best strategy is not to play the game of which round, but to submit your application as soon as, but not until, it is ready. Recently, I spoke with a client who believes she can raise her GMAT from 650 to 700, but it will mean waiting until round 2 to submit applications. My advice? Go for the 700 in round 2. Always make sure all aspects of your application are the strongest they can possibly be, and then submit. Never sacrifice quality just to get into round 1.

Final rounds for a given school (be it round 3 or round 4) are often a bad strategy. For many schools, this is the time they are focused on completing their class and picking very specific profiles. In addition, if you submit an application in March and are not admitted, you do not have much time to regroup and improve your profile before reapplying in October for the next season.

For many people it is difficult to submit all applications within one round. A better strategy may be to stagger rounds—choose a few schools to target the first round, and a few more for a later round. Once you have decided on the rounds that you are going to target, you can begin to map out your timeline and the associated schedule. As with much of this process, you need to be flexible. If you find that you are facing a deadline and the application is just not ready to go, you can always submit later.

Rolling Admissions

Some programs have a rolling admissions policy. This is worth noting because it is quite different from the idea of "rounds." With rolling admissions there may only be one deadline. A school may begin accepting applications on January 15, with the final deadline of April 15. In this situation, it is important to know that while April 15 is the last day to submit, you should NOT view it as your deadline. With rolling admissions, applications are reviewed and decisions are made as applications are received. As you progress through the time window, seats in the class are continually filled. Thus, by the very last date, a high percentage of the class may already be taken up. If someone with a similar profile submitted two months before you, and a decision was made, they very well may have taken your spot. Thus, in a rolling situation, the advice is to target the earliest possible date. This does not mean that you should submit before you are ready. However, you should submit as soon as you are ready and target an early date.

CHAPTER 16

Organizing Your Application Process

After going through this process literally hundreds of times with clients, I have some firm ideas about how to organize your calendar. How much can you recycle essays from school to school? Should you work on several schools at a time? Can you apply to all six schools in round 1? While everyone's approach will differ slightly, here is an overview of what has generally worked well for my clients.

1) One school at a time. I recommend coming very close to finishing one application before moving on to the next one. If you start working on schools in parallel, you will end up unnecessarily repeating work. You make a change to one essay, you need to go back and make that change everywhere. Trust me: "version control" can be the bane of your existence if you don't manage it from the beginning.

Again, better to wait until you have that first school close to final.

2) Plan to recycle. You do not want to recycle too much, of course. Each essay needs to be completely customized to the school and to the question being asked. But if you are asked why you want your MBA five times, there is no reason why you should have to alter that answer much. Similarly, that great example about the project you spearheaded at work can be applied to several questions across schools. You should know that one school's leadership essay can be repositioned as another school's "what are you most passionate about?" essay. Many of our clients utilize a tool called the essay grid, where they can organize all of their topics across all essays for all schools. It's a great way to "get the lay of the land" and leverage the fact that you can and should recycle great stories that are important to you.

3) View your application as a whole. Don't spend too much time agonizing over a single essay until you can view it in the context of your overall application. You may have some very good essays in isolation, but your total story may be incomplete. We suggest mapping out the subjects of all essays for a given application before you start writing the very first one. Once you have laid out your topics, you can confirm that all important stories are being told and that the set of essays presents the full picture of you and tells your entire story.

4) Be open to slipping to later rounds. Depending on deadlines, planning to have all of your applications submitted in round 1 may be incredibly ambitious. Value quality over timing. As discussed earlier, make sure that the applications are ready before rushing to submit in round 1.

5) Get ready to sweat. Don't get too freaked out by the fact that this does not come easily. Take your time and be prepared to go through several drafts. It is a very rare individual who does not struggle with this process. Expecting it to come easily is setting yourself up for failure.

CHAPTER 17

Your Marketing Plan

Your Brag Sheet

When you are finally ready to begin your essays, you will need to start by planning out your story. Our clients go through a fairly structured process to help pull out key messages and stories. We start by having all clients fill out a "brag sheet." This document is the companion to your resume. If the resume is a purely professional document, the brag sheet is the opposite. It's the document that talks about who you are outside of work—it details information about your family, your interests, your hobbies, and your challenges. You can make your own brag sheet by answering questions such as:

- What languages do you speak?
- Where have you traveled?
- Does your family have any interesting traditions?
- Have you encountered any significant hardships?
- Have you published anything?

- Do you have any patents?

Etc....

Once you have dumped a bunch of information on your brag sheet, you can weed through it and select the themes that stand out. Would you define yourself as a leader? A visionary? A team player? These attributes come together to form your overall brand. Once you have four to five brand attributes, you need to back them up with something that companies such as Procter & Gamble call "reasons to believe." The "reasons to believe" are your micro-examples, or your stories. As you approach your essays, you will need very specific stories that come together to reinforce your brand. When you take out specific essay questions for a given school, you can refer to your brand document and run through the list of stories to decide which stories fit in with which essays. Many stories are flexible and can provide support for many attributes. Once you have matched these all important stories to particular essay questions, you are ready to take the plunge!

For Example:

Brand Attribute 1: *Strong Communicator*
Reasons to Believe:
1) President of public speaking club
2) Led analyst training classes at work
3) Selected as lead negotiator for three transactions this year

Brand Attribute 2: *Global Focus*
Reasons to Believe:
1) Worked in three countries over past four years
2) Family moved a lot—lived in six countries growing up

3) Speak three languages fluently
4) Career goal focuses on international expansion of existing business

For more discussion of Brand You, see Chapter 23.

Taking the Plunge: Your Application, Your Essays

Approach to Essay-Writing

Once you know your deadlines and have mapped out a timeline, once you have planned and researched and made important decisions and once the essay questions are posted, you will finally be faced with the fact that you need to take the plunge and start writing your essays.

The two of us have very different viewpoints when it comes to finally putting your ideas down on paper...or at least onto the screen of your laptop. One of us falls into the "Just do it!" camp, whereas the other favors a planned approach that manages essay word counts. We have presented both techniques here. Applicants should figure out what kind of approach works best with their thought processes, work styles, and writing abilities.

CHAPTER 18

Don't Sweat It, Write It!

As my clients crank out their initial essay drafts, many of them contact me a bit upset over the word limits being imposed on them. They insist that they are not even halfway finished, but they have completely run out of words. "It's just not possible to describe my three most substantial experiences in only 600 words!"

My advice is to forget about word count and just write the essay. Focus on getting your content together and making sure that it is very strong. I feel that too much analysis leads to paralysis. I encourage clients to force themselves to start typing, not worry about how everything comes out, and not let themselves stop until they have answered a question. Once your content is there, you would be surprised at how easy it is to cut words. Most of us tend to be extremely verbose. You can frequently keep every important point, but just articulate with far fewer words (or to repeat this sentence with 50% word count: "articulate more concisely"). You also may be forced to consider which pieces of your story are truly pertinent to answering the question. It is very easy to start telling your story and ramble off topic. Carefully examine each piece of your essay and make sure that it is really, truly relevant, as opposed to miscellaneous background information.

CHAPTER 19

The Opposite Perspective: Word Count—Plan Ahead and Avoid the Pain

I **would have written a** shorter letter, but I didn't have the time," wrote humorist Mark Twain. Whatever challenge Twain faced in writing that single letter to his friend, you will face ten times over with your cornucopia of b-school essays.

These essays are designed to be a challenge to write within the specified word count. In a way, business schools are testing your ability to concisely convey important concepts to a reader or listener, a critical skill for an MBA student. With most writers, however, conciseness is not a goal at the beginning of the writing process, but rather a product of several time-consuming rounds of gut-wrenching revisions.

I recommend that everyone manage for word count from the very beginning of their app process, well before they have started to write a bit of prose. I encourage all of my clients to assemble a list of bullet points for a specific essay concept that covers the major sections of the text and also the illustrative "micro-examples" that provide the required specificity and story-telling flavor. In general, the word count for this document should be one-quarter to one-third the length of the finished essay. It's just a rule of thumb, but it helps makes sure you don't "over-scope" your essay concepts from the outset.

In addition, people should do a "word budget" for each grouping of related bullet points. Perhaps the typical sentence length of your writing style is 20–25 words. You literally need to decide how many sentences it will take to explain a certain topic, and then compute the amount of words required.

And don't do a totally uninformative plan that reads like this: "Fifty words for the intro. Three hundred words for the body. Fifty words for the conclusion." Rather, your word budget should have this kind of specificity: "Eighty words on how I appealed to angel investors who were interested in education issues. Sixty words on how I screened the first job candidates by having them tell me a story of their favorite subject in grade school. One hundred words on how I conducted market research using an innovative online tool."

This sounds like a lot of work, but it's really not. If you have an essay topic that is just busting to be written, the ideas will flow quickly. It may take a little while to prioritize, but that is a much easier process when the concepts are still discrete bullet points and not eloquent, multilayered prose that took you three hours to write.

Plus, I have to tell you, it is a huge time sink to try to turn an 800-word essay into a 400-word answer. We're not talking about judicious pruning or even wholesale cut-and-pasting. Often, to have an essay that makes sense, an individual has to literally rewrite many of the essay's main sections from the ground up.

Marketing Yourself Through Essays

CHAPTER 20

And the Most Important Part Is…

The most important part of the application: is it the GMAT, school transcripts, essays, interview, recommendations, resume…or something else completely? Ask most admissions committee members and they will tell you that it's the sum of many parts—there is no one "most important" piece. I have heard it said that the most important part is your weakest part—in other words, everything matters. And that one weakness could throw your carefully prepared application off completely.

Your numbers can help push you into the consideration set. While a 600 GMAT or a 2.7 GPA may raise red flags at a school like Wharton, a 700 and a 3.5 make you a solid, reasonable applicant. However, your numbers cannot get you in. Average or above-average numbers will not push you over the edge at a top school. Even an 800 and a 4.0 can meet rejection.

Although it is hard to assign "most important" status to

any one component, I will tell you that while strong essays, recommendations, and interview can provide context for low numbers, the reverse is not true. Strong numbers will never compensate for weak written materials or a sloppy, negative recommendation.

So, which component is most important? I doubt that any admissions committee would formally back me up, but I would have to cast my vote for essays being the most important aspect that the applicant creates. (This does not include recommendations, which an applicant manages but does not draft.) The essays are where the admissions committee will truly get to know you. It's where you reveal why you want to attend and differentiate yourself from all of the other 700's in the pool (and there are plenty of them!). The essays are your opportunity to present your strengths, explain your weaknesses, and generally convince them that they want you in their class.

The essays are also uniform across an entire group, so in that way they are "easier" to evaluate and compare. Interviews are all different—some conducted over the phone, some on campus, by all different types of peoples with different interview styles. Recommendations vary as well. While all candidates do their best to find great recommenders, some individuals work with MBA's who "get" the process. Others work with individuals who do not speak English and who have no idea what the MBA is. Others have a hard time finding strong recommenders because they are self-employed or work for a family business. The essays are each applicant's opportunity to present his or her true self. All applicants are given the same set of questions, and are reviewed by the same group of people, creating a level playing field, which can simplify the review.

CHAPTER 21

What Do I Need To Know About These Schools?

All of my clients ask me this question as they prepare to write the "Why MBA?" essay that most applications require. Adding school-specific details is certainly a must…but let's not get ahead of ourselves.

First, and most importantly, you need to know enough about these schools to know if you even want to apply. Don't leave it to the *Business Week* rankings to decide for you. A lot of people forget this: you are the customer! They are tweaking their programs, printing cutting-edge brochures, and traveling from city to city to convince you—the prospective MBA—to consider their schools. Each MBA application will cost you a couple of hundred bucks and dozens of hours, so make sure the programs have most of the big and the little things you want from a school. We discuss initial school research in detail in Chapter 7.

So, on to what you need to include in your essays. I can't tell you how many first drafts I've read that cite the "unmatched student body, world-class faculty, and committed alumni network" as the reasons this particular applicant has chosen a certain MBA program. This person has said nothing. You need to get specific to demonstrate that you've taken time out to research the school and that you have some legitimate reasons why you think their program fits with your needs. But don't hold yourself to too high a standard here; you're not going to blow the committee away with some statement that shows you are the figurative "soul mate" of their MBA program ("My God, when she mentioned our emphasis on entrepreneurship, I just knew she had to be a part of our Columbia Business School community," said the director of admissions as he wiped a tear of joy away from his cheek. "I knew it…I knew it!").

You can effectively research schools in just a few minutes (of course, you'll have to dive in deeper in preparation for interviews, but that's another topic). Check out the following offerings/traits of the school to see in what ways they mesh with your professional goals, learning agenda, personality, and preferences:

- Program format: case vs. lecture, traditional vs. accelerated, opportunities for study abroad, opportunities for "hands-on learning"
- Academic offerings: specific classes in your areas of interest (don't make a laundry list; find a couple and show how they might impact you)
- Faculty: certain specific profs that you might want meet with, help with research, etc.
- Initiatives: often schools will emphasize certain disciplines or issues for several years, hosting events, developing new classes, etc. These are dubbed names "The Entrepreneurship Program," "The Healthcare ative," or "The Technology Roundtable."

- Field studies: faculty support for independent research, business plan development, etc.
- Cross-registration opportunities: what other resources does this university have to offer?
- Clubs

Four to six sentences of solid material on "Why our program?" should set you up nicely. Remember, you usually will have tons of other material to cover about your career progress and other topics, so no need to go on and on telling them about themselves.

CHAPTER 22

Be Part of the Solution: Know Yourself and the "Needs" of Your Schools

One key to business school admissions success is understanding that you are marketing yourself to a school just as a product is marketed to a consumer in the grocery store. The school is your target market. By understanding the school's "needs," you can successfully position yourself as part of the solution. For example, consider Columbia Business School. Located in the heart of NYC, and well known for its finance curriculum, you can imagine that they receive many applications from individuals wanting to launch a career in finance. Columbia, however, is also interested in being known as a top general management program. Columbia is looking for well-rounded leaders, entrepreneurs, managers, marketers, innovators, and more. As you submit your Columbia application, think hard about what they may "need" to round out their incoming class and try to become part of the solution.

This is true for all schools: in order to be successful, at some point you should step away from your needs. Think about the school's goals and needs and how you can contribute to fulfilling those needs. For example, they probably want involved students, committed alumni, active volunteers and more. When you finish telling the admissions committee why you want to attend and what they can do for you, don't forget to show them what you can do for them as well.

CHAPTER 23

Developing "Brand You": The Way to Drive Home Your Main Points

Think for a moment about the audience for your business school application: you will be spending hour upon hour writing a magnum opus that may be read by just one person—or a select few at most. These people have dozens of applications they need to get through each day and even the most diligent may at times miss some points in your essays. That's why you need to make things as easy as possible for the admissions committee members by making sure they can't miss who you are and what you can add to the class.

The best applications feature four or five aspects of the applicant's character and experiences that anyone reading the essays can't help but identify. These four to five traits combine to form "Brand You."

We all know the power of brands. Companies spend tons of cash to make sure you know how they deliver value and what they stand for. While there are many more subtle facets to their full corporate identities and many nuances to their product/service offerings, firms need to make sure that customers have a complete and unambiguous understanding of a limited list of characteristics. Take, for instance, this list of traits for a few well-know companies:

1. Low prices everyday, huge selection, one-stop shop
2. Great place to hang out, socially responsible, respect for employees
3. Great design, simplifying the complex, cool
4. Irreverent, youth-oriented, influencing lifestyles
5. Fun, family, fantasy

Even from just these short descriptions, you can probably guess which companies we're referencing (see below). That's because these messages have been pounded into your head through repetition, multiple interactions with the firm, or exposure to marketing messages.

Similarly, candidates need to make sure the people who read their applications make no mistake about the core of their character and experiences. Certainly, all applications end up covering more than three to four points if they capture the wonderful complexities of us as humans. But if we give equal weight to 20 traits, we water down the main features the admissions committee needs to understand about us.

If a candidate wants to be known as "a natural leader... intellectual, creative, driven, community-minded, responsible, action-oriented, nurturing, committed, rigorous, internationally focused, physically fit, welcoming, laid back, institution-building, and adventurous," ultimately, we really don't know what this person stands for.

However, people "branding" themselves like this have made real choices on what they want to emphasize:

"A behind-the-scenes leader, creative problem-solver, and passionate about international development."

"A great motivator, cutting-edge thinker on financial markets, and committed to education."

"Dedicated to environmental causes, a skilled negotiator, a committed mentor, and family-oriented."

Reinforce the main three to four traits through repetition; other aspects of your character and experience will come out naturally.

It's never too early to start cogitating on the general outlines and topics for your essays. Paying attention to what makes a "great essay" months before you start writing will help you sort through your best concepts.

Just a few words can trigger our thoughts about a brand. Did you get these from the short statements above?
1. Wal-Mart
2. Starbucks
3. Apple
4. MTV
5. Disney

CHAPTER 24

How Am I Different?

Consider this profile of a business school applicant:

- 3.7 GPA from Duke
- 730 GMAT
- 3 years in investment banking at Goldman Sachs
- YMCA Young Adult Board Member

On the surface, most would agree that this sounds like a great applicant. And she is a great applicant—solid essays, strong recommendations, a polished presentation in her interview. The only problem is that she is competing against all of her fellow all-star Goldman analysts, as well as analysts at other top banks.

Top schools are seeking diversity. No matter how excellent, they will not accept all candidates with similar profiles. If you are in this boat, one question weighing on your mind is probably how to set yourself apart from the rest of the talent in the applicant pool. Fortunately, because the essays play an important role in this process, the resume details featured above are just the beginning. In your essays you have a great opportunity to let your unique voice come through and demonstrate how you are different from your competition. It is these details that can truly make a difference for you.

You may have the same basic job description as many others, but what did you do with that job? Were you promoted? How did you find better ways to accomplish tasks? Did you act as a mentor? Were you a leader? Did you propose great ideas? How did you gain the respect of others?

Setting yourself apart does not mean learning to play the piano with one hand. Examples that may feel less than extraordinary to you can actually provide the admissions committee with evidence of your excellence. One client, working as a strategy consultant, could not fit traditional volunteer work into his crazy travel schedule. He took it upon himself to reach out to his alma mater's career center and offer to be a unique resource to those interested in a consulting career. He ended up giving back from a distance, on his own hours, but in a very significant way. He is currently at Wharton.

When thinking about how to differentiate, don't get frustrated if you do not have a building named after you, or if you have not won an Olympic medal. Excellence can come in smaller packages, and these small examples are the best way to showcase your individuality and unique contributions.

Here are some examples that clients actually wanted to omit from their applications because they did not find them particularly special or perhaps relevant to business school. However, they were extremely important to the individual's overall story and added color and depth to their profiles.

1) Black belt in karate
2) Grew up sailing with family
3) Launched a recruiting program for students at his alma later
4) Inspired co-workers to contribute to company-wide fundraising efforts
5) Used basic Excel to simplify manual entry of data in standard company processes
6) Developed a great network of personal relationships throughout her life

"Joe Business" vs. "Jack of All Trades": How to Bring Out Your Human Side Without Looking Like a Dilettante

Yes, you're applying to business school, but you don't need to look like a business tool.

If you've doubled sales, you need to discuss that. If you've helped get a new technology to market, you need to write about that. If you've hired a hundred people, you've got a great story there.

However, I've seen too many candidates who attempt to make it look like they've done it all already. They believe by demonstrating their business acumen in every paragraph of their applications, the sheer weight of the evidence of their commercial genius will overwhelm the admissions committee. Not the best approach.

One candidate I worked with received numerous rejections two years earlier in spite of solid work experience and stellar GMAT scores. We attributed his early failure to his "gunner" approach to his application. When we developed his human side more last year, his admissions fortunes rose considerably.

MBA programs emphasize that they choose their classes based on their potential for leadership going forward. Often, that leadership will be in the arena of policy, public health, the arts, not-for-profits, etc. Admissions committees look for people who have followed their passions and left a unique mark in whatever areas they have pursued. The books that have most influenced the best MBA candidates are not necessarily just by Jim Collins, Warren Buffett, and Geoffrey Moore. The current issues that impact them the most are not just tax code debates and the state of global outsourcing.

On the other end of the spectrum, some MBA candidates try to fashion themselves as Renaissance men and women who would put Leonardo da Vinci to shame. Sometimes, it's hard to figure out how a person can get any PowerPoint slides done with all of the oil painting, tutoring, skiing, sky diving, Farsi speaking, flower arranging, foreign film watching, blogging, environment saving, meal delivering, judo-ing, and overseas traveling he engages in every week.

The best way to develop the "human side" of the application is to take just a couple of experiences, activities, or themes, and develop them in a much more detailed and nuanced way. Instead of an essay that deals with ten foreign travel experiences in a cursory way, develop one or two anecdotes in more depth. Talk about the way one trip or one discussion with someone from another country changed the way you viewed the world. Discuss one observation you have had about a certain topic across different cultures. Maybe you've witnessed differences in communication or distinct ways various cultures view entrepreneurship. Illustrating that you understand the significance of certain things you've experienced is much more important than regaling an admissions committee with all of the experiences.

One candidate I worked with put down "chess" as an interest on his app. He had read somewhere that many successful executives cited chess as their favorite game. He had played a few times and enjoyed it, so saw no problem listing it as one of his interests. I asked him, "What happens if your interviewer is a real chess devotee? Are you going to have anything to tell him about it he'll find at all interesting?" There is no ideal list of interests that will make someone seem more appealing to b-school admissions committees. If your interest is reading pop fiction, maybe it has allowed you to bond with your friends in book club. This is in itself an insight about you that can lead to further discussions. If your interest is baseball trivia, maybe it gives you an interesting perspective on some of the race and drug issues that the sport has experienced. Don't shy away from your true interests; illustrate how they have helped shape the incredibly dynamic and fascinating person that you are!

Your Essays:
Important Themes

Showing Leadership

CHAPTER 26

What Is Leadership?

You're going to need to figure out the answer to this question very, very soon. Some applications have explicit questions about your defining leadership experiences. While others don't boast a "leadership" question per se, the best applications will serve up a heavy dose of this particular "L word" in other essays on personal achievements, passions, etc.

Applicants need to think through their past experiences to find the episodes that best illustrate their leadership skills. Sometimes, the best examples are not the first that come to mind. Many applicants automatically tag some of their greatest personal achievements as perfect examples of leadership. However, this is not always the best formula for a strong leadership essay.

Just because you achieved something outstanding does not always mean leadership skills were involved, especially if you did most or all of the work. The work of the leader activates or improves the work of others; find anecdotes in your work and extracurricular history that illustrate this kind of pattern.

What kind of experiences will make the best tales of leadership? Think about challenges where the following came into play:

- Identifying/defining a problem
- Articulating a vision
- Resisting conventional approaches; challenging status quo
- Convincing others of importance of problem
- Marshaling resources to address problem
- Motivating others
- Making good use of others' talents
- Being open to new information, input, etc.
- Building consensus with appropriate stakeholders
- Guiding strong mid-course corrections; overcoming mistakes
- Building on success
- Permanently upgrading organization's capabilities; institutionalizing solution
- Illustrating methods for other individuals, organizations, etc.

And remember: leadership is not just about the titles. Some candidates build their leadership essays around the fact that they were selected for or elected to certain positions where they had a high level of authority and responsibility: editor-in-chief of a college paper, fraternity president, captain of the hockey team, director of product development, V.P. of marketing, etc. But what did you do with this position? An editor of a college daily could write about how she was constantly challenged to maintain high levels of editorial excellence, manage staff assignments, and hit all deadlines. This is definitely an esteemed position with tons of responsibility, but Ms. Editor, if you describe your role like that, it sounds exactly the same as the role of the other 798 editors-in-chief of college papers. Define the leadership challenges you faced, not the management challenges. Did you have to deal with a certain writer who falsified interview notes? Was there a sticky campus scandal that forced you and your staff to walk an ethical tightrope? Did you have to fire student editors? Did you lead a transition from a weekly to a daily with all of the scheduling and human resources rigors that entails?

Collecting impressive titles does not make someone a great leader—helping a team overcome great challenges does.

Proving "managerial" potential

Munish
U MICHIGAN. ROSS

Not having any direct reports, plus, being from a very over-subscribed pool of applicants—Indian engineers—was definitely a concern to me. One thing that really helped me shine in my leadership essays was reading the [preceding chapter] about "what is leadership" and detailing ways you can show leadership without having direct reports in your job. I focused on my extra-curriculars, highlighting my experience as president of the local Toastmasters Club.

Omar
CORNELL

My main challenge was that I didn't have that "traditional" work experience: graduating and then going to a good firm and working as an analyst for two years before business school. I had to convince the admissions committee that the things I did [military service and then independent real estate development and investing] were as good if not better than their traditional applicants.

I had started a bunch of side businesses and projects. But I was told that I really had to focus on just one of those, otherwise my overall story would get lost. It would look like I just jumped around. I think that was an extremely useful tip.

As a veteran, I would say people with military experience should definitely emphasize it a lot, but not make it the exclusive focus of their application. But I've seen some applications from military people where they go on and on, page after page, and every example is from the military. It makes you wonder if they had any experiences or perspective from outside the military. Do you know anything else about life? Are you really a good fit or are you too stuck in the military perspective? Don't overdo it!

CHAPTER 27

Leadership and Accomplishments: Two Very Different Types of Essays

You gotta love the b-school application process. For most of us, it will be the final time in our lives where someone lets us brag on and on about ourselves—and will actually read what we write and listen to what we have to say.

But as fun as this bragging process can be, let's make sure we brag about the right things. Some applicants don't focus their essays properly when it comes to their accomplishment and leadership essays. Many folks view these as nearly interchangeable essays, but they definitely require different approaches.

One of the central tenets of leadership essays is showing that you can enable the actions of other people. You bring out their passions. You educate them. You help them see organizational priorities in new ways. And then they share in the achievement.

Accomplishment essays can include leadership experiences, but there are many scenarios applicants recount in the "leadership" essays that really do not belong under that heading. As I stated earlier, just because you did something great does not mean leadership was involved. Some people try to get around this issue by inserting the tried and true "I led by example" gambit. They write about some really cool thing that they accomplished on their own and then assert that it was actually an episode where they inspired others who had the privilege of basking in the glow of this tremendous achievement. If one of your essays portrays you as a lone warrior undertaking a noble quest until the final paragraph when you play the "leading by example" card, you have missed the boat.

The best leadership essays will have heroes other than yourself. If you helped Terri in accounts receivable realize her full potential on a project you led, showcase her as a hero in your leadership tale.

In the best of all worlds, people create a good balance between these types of essays at the beginning of their application process, even before they commence writing. The good news is that, in many instances, you can adjust your application fairly late in the process to achieve the appropriate balance between individual achievement and leadership. Insert a few sentences here and there about enabling others, or educating and defining priorities for group endeavors. Many achievement essays can be transformed into glorious examples of leadership when you shine the spotlight on others who were a part of a great collective accomplishment.

Writing About the Future: Your Career and Why You Need an MBA

Your Future Career Path: Whether It's Definite or Undecided, Get Ready to Write About It

Many candidates see business school as a great opportunity to figure out what sort of career path they want to pursue in the future. MBA programs tout their career services departments as excellent places to find information about a variety of industries and jobs. They hype their alumni networks as great resources for getting the inside scoop on certain careers and companies. And they promote the b-school summer internship as an opportunity to "test drive" any new sort of occupation you are considering.

So, since business school is a place of reflection on careers, can applicants just put a big fat "TBD" in the essay where they discuss their career goals?

Not a chance.

Even if you view b-school as your figurative mountaintop retreat for career path contemplation, your business school application needs to set forth a fairly definite plan of what you would want to do with your degree. Don't worry—they won't limit your course offerings based on your stated career goals or withhold your diploma if you deviate from your essay when actually choosing your career.

MBA programs basically want to know that you'll make good use of one of the limited spots in their classes. From personal experience, I can tell you that people who have a "learning agenda" related to their chosen career path are more impressive academically and generally have achieved more in their first few years out of school.

You don't need to get incredibly specific—and as a matter of fact it might sound contrived if you focus in on a certain company (e.g., "I want to be a consultant in McKinsey's San Francisco office"). However, you should have an "opportunity set" that appeals to you (e.g., "I want to be in a consulting role where I can work on critical technology issues. I love the variety and learning opportunity consulting offers.").

If you plan on making a fairly significant transition from your current career path, refer to the specific experiences that spurred the change. A banker who wishes to get into marketing post b-school may mention that his favorite project dealt with consumer products. A consultant who wishes to follow an entrepreneurial path may point out the fun she had running a business while in college. Et cetera, et cetera.

The essay writing process is a great opportunity in itself to reflect on your goals. After all, you may have to pick a school in part based on specialties they might possess in certain disciplines. Plus, you'll be all the more convincing in your essays and interviews if you've thought through at least one possible career path in great detail.

CHAPTER 29

Demonstrating the Need: Show How Much You Value This Degree

As you fill out your business school applications, you will undoubtedly encounter some very challenging essay questions. To be successful, you will go through a lot of soul searching and self-discovery. Most applicants are bound to encounter the "why MBA" question frequently. It is surprising how difficult this relatively straightforward question can be. Applicants who have focused goals and defined reasons for wanting to apply often still struggle.

Demonstrating that you will benefit from the experience offered by your target program is critical to your success. Even if you are not asked the question explicitly, you should be aware that your story needs to illustrate that the program can help you achieve your personal and professional goals.

Every year, I work with reapplicants who solicit feedback on applications they submitted in prior years. Here are some highlights from recent feedback sessions that illustrate the point above:

Applicant A:

> GPA - 3.9
> GMAT - 680
> Experience - 2 years' strategy consulting
> Goal - CTO of a global organization

Feedback—not clear why you need an MBA. Seems like your goals are more technical than managerial.

Applicant B:

> GPA - 3.1
> GMAT - 710
> Experience - 4 years' venture capital
> Goal - continuing current career in venture capital

Feedback—not clear why you want an MBA. Seems that you are gaining relevant experience on the job. What can the MBA provide?

Applicant C:

> GPA - 3.6
> GMAT - 700
> Experience - 3 years' strategy consulting
> Goal - career in arts management

Feedback—not clear why you need an MBA; the degree is generally not required for Arts Management.

The moral of all of this is—make sure it is clear to the admissions committee that the MBA can help you reach your stated goals in a very specific way. Understand what you will gain from their program and communicate that clearly to them. Do not be discouraged by the examples above. Each one of these applicants was ultimately successful. They did not change their basic stories, just the way they told them. Your explanation should demonstrate an understanding of what an MBA can provide, and the benefits of their specific program. This can also include insights into their culture, and ways that being immersed in that environment can help you develop.

CHAPTER 30

Show You Mean Business About Business SCHOOL: Be Specific About Your "Learning Agenda"

"You want to go to business school? So what do you want to learn?"

It seems a simple enough inquiry, but applicants often have a very difficult time responding to it. When we went to college, interviewers might ask us about our intended major, but we could craft a pretty broad answer.

In business school, we're ALL business majors, so we have to have a more defined message to stand out. It's not enough to say, "I want to learn more about accounting, finance, and marketing." You will, indeed, learn about those subjects. And so will the hundreds of other folks who enter with you. They're called "Required Courses," after all.

Instead of painting with a broad brush, you will need to put a finer point on things in order to prove that you are a serious applicant who has determined that business school is THE logical next step in a career progression. To some people, business school is just a rite of passage or a brand name to add to the resume. But remember, there are people at b-schools who are spending thousands of man-hours developing course materials and standing in front of semi-comatose students, all in the name of "learning." So, you had better know what you want to learn.

If you have a certain "spike" or element of strength in your candidacy, you may choose to develop it further. You may have worked in marketing for the last four years, but realize you want to further your knowledge of youth brand building and unconventional sales channel development because of a certain entrepreneurial idea you have, for instance.

Or, you may have areas you've identified as gaps in your professional skillset. Perhaps you've been an investment banker for three years and have developed a deep understanding of valuation and debt finance. But, in order to be a part of the LBO industry after b-school, you want to shore up your skills analyzing industrial operations or navigating business law.

Think about the kinds of articles you click to online, or the ones you tear out of *Fortune* or *Business* 2.0 to read later. Talking about those kinds of topics will lead you to develop sections of essays and answers to interview questions that are compelling and well-researched. You may want to introduce your interests in an essay like this:

- "I'm fascinated by the ways brands like Apple have been rolled out in new markets and foreign cultures."
- "I have seen the power of internal incentives on organizational behavior and I want to understand them as a management tool."
- "I'm impressed by the way top-flight organizations like Starbucks are able to maintain their high levels of customer service."

- "In an interconnected world, I want to learn how supply chains can be a competitive advantage."

Coming up with a short list of subjects that fascinate you can help you research course offerings, research initiatives, and clubs at the schools of your choice.

Think about your learning agenda in terms of:

- Subject areas: More specific than "marketing." We mean "brand development," "channel creation," or "pricing."
- Methodologies: Not "financial modeling," but rather "valuation techniques" or "earnings forecasting."
- Industries: Technology, health care, or consumer products. Better yet, get a little more specific with market segments like "security technologies," "new health care service models," or "branded luxury products." These are still mega-billion-dollar industries with plenty of opportunities for innovation.
- Geographies: Are you well-versed in organizational behavior as applied to U.S. companies? Well, maybe you want to learn about the differences in India, the Middle East, or Latin America. Or maybe you want to learn about investing in China or Canada. You will have plenty of classmates and case materials to help you learn about these different economies.

How to Talk About the "Bad Stuff"

CHAPTER 31

Turning Weakness into Strength

One of the most dreaded questions asked by business schools is, "Discuss your weaknesses." It can feel like a double-edged sword: you have to come up with an honest answer, but you are afraid to reveal too much. You have just expended a ton of energy trying to prove you are fantastic and now you need to reveal weakness. My advice here: be as brutally honest as possible. Through your honesty, you are actually revealing a strength: self-awareness. Self-awareness is key to growth and success—and to being admitted to business school.

Discussing weakness is a time to really showcase all of who you are and allow the admissions committee to get to know the real you, including some vulnerability. You can stop trying to be a superhero and reveal your humanity. One weakness essay I reviewed was powerful because the applicant discussed his struggle with public speaking that linked back to a speech impediment he had as a child. He discussed his journey, which included surgeries and speech therapy as a young child. As an adult, his speaking was just fine, but his confidence level was not where he wanted it to be. He had identified improving his public speaking skills as a priority and was steadily working towards his goal.

Honest introspection allows the admissions committee to get to know you. And, let's be honest, if you were "perfect" and already had the full tool set, would you really be shelling out thousands of dollars to spend two years in business school? Discussing weakness with honesty and maturity is the key to turning weakness into strength.

CHAPTER 32

Weak Examples of Weakness

Many schools will ask you or your recommenders, or both, to discuss weaknesses or areas for improvement. This can be difficult because you are walking the fine line between being honest and exposing too much. Here, as in the rest of the application, honest introspection can lead to the best answers. There are as many valid weaknesses and developmental needs as there are people. However, there are some approaches that are overused and ineffective and just don't work. The following summarizes the top four "bad ways to address the weakness question."

1) A weakness that is really a strength: "I am a perfectionist who works too hard to get everything right."

2) A weakness that you have already addressed completely, for example in this recommendation: "Jason was a poor public speaker, but after I discussed this with him, he joined a public speaking club, read

several books on the subject, and worked hard to improve. Since then, he has become one of the strongest speakers in the company."

3) A claim that you have no weaknesses.

4) A weakness that will be totally cured merely by attending business school: "My biggest weakness is my need for formal finance training. An MBA from Stanford will definitely resolve this issue."

While claiming that the weakness is cured does not answer the question effectively, showing that you are aware of it and working to address it is fair. Returning to the public speaking example above: "Jason's public speaking skills can be improved upon. He and I discussed this issue a couple of months ago and I was impressed that his response was to join a public speaking club. Since then he has volunteered to present on several occasions and I have seen some improvement in his skills." Discussing your plan to further address the weakness in business school is also an important tactic.

This is one of the most difficult questions to answer because of a fear of being too honest, but true self-awareness is critical to success in MBA admissions. Trying to come off as perfect may actually be a window to your greatest flaw.

Weaknesses: Fair and Balanced Reporting Gains You Cred

During this essay-writing process we get to praise ourselves, to brag, to point out our unique understanding of complex issues and just generally paint ourselves as the ideal human. But in order to balance out the admissions karma, we also have to give ourselves a couple of body slams by critiquing our own skills, motivations, etc.

Kellogg has in some years asked candidates to provide an "evaluative assessment" of their own file. I've seen some candidates riddle themselves with critique after critique. In their minds, they thought "assessment" really meant to "point out all of your weaknesses." They become their own worst Simon Cowells. Don't make this mistake. We can assess both the strengths and the negatives. When you include an honest assessment of your negatives, you gain credibility for any strengths you raise.

Harvard has also asked candidates to critique their own

leadership abilities in the same essays they recount their leadership strengths. Some candidates wax eloquent about an unmitigated victory for their leadership skills and then chime in with a fairly minor critique. Often, this critique is totally unrelated to the narrative of the leadership tale they've just recounted. The best stories for this essay usually have a couple of bumps on the road to leadership that we could have avoided if not for our blindspots; in essence, the weakness makes the leadership challenge more significant and, hence, the leadership tale even more intriguing. And make sure to relate this critique to the elements of leadership described in Chapter 26 (defining agendas, communicating, inspiring, managing up, etc.); don't make yourself out to be a master motivator and then merely critique your Excel modeling skills.

CHAPTER 34

Weakness and Failure— Related Yet Different

In addition to being asked about your weaknesses, you are just as likely to be asked about a time that you have failed. While these questions may be equally dreaded, they are quite different and the answers are generally not interchangeable. A failure essay will generally summarize a situation where things did not go as planned. You might well reveal a personal weakness or two in the story, but the "failure" is the distinct event. You can then proceed to write about what you learned and hopefully how you have incorporated this knowledge into your performance going forward. When you discuss a failure, you might be part of a team that failed. If that is the case, be careful not to "pass the buck" and blame the team or the manager. You need to take responsibility, at least in part, in order to show that you have learned and moved on.

In contrast, a weakness is not an event, it is one or more qualities that you possess on an ongoing basis that can be improved upon. Forgive me for feeling the need to define a pretty basic word in our vocabulary, but I cannot tell you how many weakness essays discuss an event…or how many failure essays actually discuss personal weaknesses.

Just as discussing weakness can reveal strength, candidly speaking about failure can be key to your business school success. Last year, I had a client who was laid off three times throughout his four-year career. He was terrified of revealing this to the admissions committees. However, when he finally did talk about these failures, he also demonstrated self-awareness and an ability to learn from his mistakes and the mistakes of others. He showed maturity, resilience, determination, and a whole host of qualities that business schools are looking for. Ultimately, this applicant was not only admitted to a top five school, but also received a prestigious scholarship!

In addition to asking about failures or weaknesses, some applications may inquire about setbacks that you have experienced. The examples you use here may be quite distinct from the other categories. For example, the death of a close relative, an illness, or other personal issues may lead to a failure such as a low GPA one quarter. These examples constitute setbacks, but an illness, for example, would not be considered a weakness. Be aware of these slight innuendos in the language of your essay questions. Following directions and answering specifically what is asked is critical. The admissions committees are looking for specific information and answering a question that is not there is a sure way to lose points.

Addressing Sensitive Topics in Your Essays

Beyond **actually fessing up** to failures and weaknesses, the essays are a forum to provide an explanation for aspects of your background that require clarification or of which you are not terribly proud. You will have to decide case by case what warrants an explanation, but you should not ever assume that the admissions committee will gloss over some aspect of your background, or that other strengths will erase a weak spot. If a glaring weakness exists, they will see it. And if an explanation is not provided, they may jump to their own conclusions. As you provide explanations, you should consider why the admissions committee cares about a certain aspect of the application and work to allay their concerns. For example, there are very good reasons why GPA is important. Beyond proving that you can handle rigorous academics, your GPA provides insight into your work ethic, multi-tasking skills, commitment to excellence, and track record of success.

Think about how you can address some of these concerns through your story.

Low GPA: We discussed this a bit in our earlier section on candidacy. In addition to taking a class to demonstrate that you can handle a challenging quantitative curriculum, you may want to provide some context for why your grades suffered during undergraduate studies. Here it is important to be very clear on the difference between providing background and making excuses. Explaining that your grades were poor because the curriculum was really difficult is generally not going to fly. The business schools consider their curriculum to be challenging as well! However, you may be able to explain that your grades dipped due to some personal challenges, a family emergency, a health crisis, or more. This is also where honesty can be most effective. If the reason for low grades is lack of focus or immaturity, own up to it and show how you have changed. Don't dwell on it—and move on. Note that one slightly low grade probably does not necessitate an explanation. Use judgment regarding where you dedicate time to explaining a downfall in your application, and do not feel the need to detail reasons for every small hiccup in your background.

Taking extra time to graduate college: There are many reasons why one may have taken extra time to graduate from college. Often, these reasons and explanations can be very interesting reflections of your interests and allow the admissions committee to learn more about what you were pursuing at that time in your life. It can certainly be okay to take that extra time, especially if you have a compelling reason for doing so. If you took time off to be a ski bum, or temporarily drop out, this is another time when you may need to be honest and own up to a lack of focus, then provide evidence of a more recent shift in priorities.

Switching majors: Some applicants want to explain a drastic shift in majors and it often makes sense to do so. While changing majors is not necessarily a weakness, it can raise questions about your focus, or at the very least, leave the admissions committee curious about the change. An honest depiction of why you decided to change is called for. There may be an interesting event that led to the change or just a gradual shift in interests. College is a time for discovery and learning about oneself. Being honest about your evolution can be an interesting way for an admissions committee to learn more about your interests.

When you appear unfocused

"I abruptly switched majors."

Andrew
HARVARD

I started out undergrad as a pre-med student, and spent three years taking tons of science courses. I then made an abrupt change my senior year and decided to pursue a career in business. I felt that it required explanation, as I abandoned the major I had invested a lot in and piled up on business courses. I think that college is about exploring new areas, so it was not a terrible thing, but I did want to justify all of the time that I spent focused on med classes and internships, and also bring some light into my decision to turn to business. Finally, since I applied to school just one year out of college, I wanted the admissions committees to understand that I was truly serious about my new direction and it was not just a fickle decision on my part. As I thought through this

issue I felt that the key to making the admissions committees understand the steps I had taken was explaining how I became inspired to operate in the business world and show that my interest in medicine had not disappeared, only changed a bit. I discussed my introduction to the role that business could play in many fields, including medicine, and how I felt that management skills were critical to helping me reach my goals. I also tied these goals to the healthcare industry. Thus, I felt that I had a pretty cohesive story in the end.

Because my one year of work experience was very much removed from healthcare, I decided to get involved with a volunteer organization that supported health issues – mostly related to immunizations. When I first looked at my "story" it appeared to be a very drastic change from medicine to something completely unrelated. But as I worked through the details of my goals, I was truly able to tie it altogether which I think lent credibility to my desire to switch gears and pursue an MBA.

Low GMAT: This is a tough one to "explain." Since all applicants take the same test under the same circumstances, and you are allowed to retake the test as frequently as you like, it is difficult to come up with a good reason for why you cannot hit that 700. What you can do, however, is leave little question regarding your academic abilities by proving competence elsewhere. Perhaps your undergraduate GPA erases some of the concerns. Perhaps challenging quantitative courses that you have taken more recently will satisfy the admissions committee's concerns. A job that is quantitatively rigorous and recommenders who testify to your skills may also appease the committee. The GMAT is just one way to measure competence, and while it is important, if you cannot hit a target score, you can certainly find other ways to demonstrate your skills.

In some instances, such as the Kellogg question that asks you to discuss your candidacy, it may make sense to point out that you are a "poor test taker." However, you would not need to devote an essay to this topic, as there is not all that much to say here. Admissions can see from your score that you are a poor test taker, and if you provide evidence of other skills, at least they will not also conclude that you are weak in other areas.

No outside activities: A dearth of outside activities can make an individual appear one dimensional and not terribly interesting. Even if you have no obvious candidates for this category, dig deep and really think about how you have spent your time. Many applicants think that they have done nothing worth mentioning but don't realize how intriguing an interest in the martial arts, a trip to Uganda, or organizing a company soccer league can be. If you truly have nothing to speak of outside of work, you are going to have to strive that much harder to reveal your personality through anecdotes from work or personal interactions. Be very careful about making excuses regarding a lack of volunteer work. Everyone is busy, but somehow, lots of people find the time.

Lots of career changes: If you have a high volume of job changes on your resume, you may appear to lack commitment or be unfocused. You will probably need to explain the reason for your changes and help the admissions committee to understand the motivation behind your decisions. It's important in this situation to refrain from merely chronicling your resume. You will want to explain the "WHY?" behind the "WHAT you did." There is no right number of jobs, or right number of years at a job. Most important is to explain why each step is a logical one in your path to the MBA and longer term goals. If there was a misstep somewhere, you can explain what happened, how you corrected course, and what you learned. This can also add important dimension to your application.

A less than cohesive resume

"I had an erratic career path."

Aldys
U MICHIGAN, ROSS

I worked for five years before applying to business school and jumped around a lot professionally during this time. My undergraduate degree was in American Civilization, which did not really lend itself to a high-powered job straight out of school. The truth is that I did not really know exactly what I wanted to do either. As a result, I switched around a lot and had three jobs before going to business school.

At the time I wrote my applications, it was three jobs in four years and they were very different jobs – really I felt that there was no true career progression. I started out in an advertising agency, then went on to work in product marketing for a start-up and finally ended up in a non-profit doing very hands-on operational  work. This created two problems for me. First of all, I was afraid that I would seem very unfocused and schizophrenic. I had no real reason for taking the first two jobs except that they seemed interesting and fun, but I certainly was not thinking about my broader career vision. I did not know how to tell a cohesive story about my prior experience and how this would link to my future goals (which to tell you the truth were also a bit fuzzy at the time I applied). Second of all, by switching around a lot I always started over in an entry-level position, and four years later was essentially at the bottom. I first had to learn the ropes in advertising, then product marketing and then the non-profit world. So I had experienced quite a bit and learned quite a bit but none of it was really inter-related and I was still pretty much at the bottom of my game.

When it came time to work on my essays, I looked at all of my experience and tried to find a common theme. The theme that emerged was marketing. Although that was not really the way I had planned it. I did learn one aspect of marketing working at an advertising agency. I also had a very customer focused role in product marketing. Finally, in my role at the non-profit I wore many hats and did help out with some marketing and general outreach initiatives. Once I discovered this common thread it seemed so obvious and it all flowed quite naturally. I was able to tell a clear story and also link it into my goals. In addition, identifying this theme really helped me to address the question of, "how did I grow in my career?" because I could talk about how my knowledge of marketing had grown. I pointed out examples of how I was leading some of the outreach initiatives in my current role and leveraging what I had learned in advertising and product. The end result was a story that actually flowed and wow—I seemed like I had actually had a plan in mind. And I suppose by just following my interests I did have a sort of plan in mind. I am truly interested in marketing as a career so perhaps that is what was guiding me all along!

Lacking obvious career progression: Some candidates find it hard to illustrate professional growth when their job title has not changed in many years. However, a formal promotion is just one way to demonstrate that you have developed your skills. In this case, you and your recommenders will have to work even harder to show that your abilities and responsibilities have grown within the context of your same position. You will need to detail projects that show advancement, and discuss ways that your role has changed over time, such as managing others or assuming responsibility for new initiatives. Your recommenders can back all of this up by detailing your growth, and discussing ways that you have developed personally. Finally, you can highlight different phases of a job, even within the same job title, by grouping responsibilities under a different set of years on your resume.

Title stagnation

"I had little formal job progression in six years."

Dana
COLUMBIA

I graduated from college six years before deciding to apply to business school, so I was above the average age for a business school student. I was worried because I felt that at my age, I had a greater burden to show that I had come a long way with my career.

My challenge was that I had been in the same job since graduating and my title had been essentially the same the entire time. I had been promoted from Product Manager to Senior Product Manager after two years and had remained at the Senior Manager level for the next four years. In this role I never had direct reports and I initially felt that it would be very difficult to convey how my responsibilities and abilities had increased over time. I did two things to mitigate this issue. First, I was very careful in my essays to demonstrate clear growth. I talked about skills that I gained and how I incorporated them at later dates. I also discussed ways that I took initiative and led projects, even in the absence of formal hierarchical authority. I did manage projects and people across functions, and my abilities and leadership skills grew a lot. I was very specific about accomplishments and how each project built upon another one. Second,

I spoke with my recommenders about this issue and asked them to explain the flat structure of our company, and detail how I had grown and increased my actual responsibilities even though my title had not changed. We talked a lot about the skills that I had developed and the responsibilities I had taken on in later years that really reflected my growth – in terms of skills and also relationships and management.

In the end, I really tried to ignore the issue of titles and do everything I could to show that the essence behind a formal title *had* changed and I had in fact grown a lot. I tried to show that I had an increased impact on the company and I believe that my recommenders backed this up with details. I think the third-party support was essential here because they could help paint the picture and it was not just me saying that titles did not mean much in my company—it was my boss and the company owner.

Being fired or laid off: A candidate may be outright fired from a job for poor performance. More frequently, however, we see applicants who are laid off due to downsizing. This often happens very early on in a job, before the applicant even has a chance to prove his- or herself in the position. As with other difficult situations, this is a time for honesty. If you have made a mistake, this is the time to own up to what happened and take responsibility for a poor decision. If you were caught by surprise early on in a job, you can explain what was learned, and demonstrate how you have bounced back from this failure or setback.

How applicants handled getting laid off

"I was laid off three times!"

David
WHARTON

I applied to business school in 2005. When I started working on my essays, I knew I had a bumpy road ahead of me because I had lost my job twice during my three-year career. Once, my company had laid off a large percentage of the company, including myself, during a standard downsizing. The second time, my company folded very abruptly after our big product launch. The biggest news was yet to come. I was laid off a third time while working on my applications, just a month before I had to submit.

This was obviously terrible news and I had no idea how to handle it in my applications. I considered not mentioning it and pretending that nothing had changed because it was only a month off. But then I thought about all of the issues—recommenders, background checks, interviews, and how I would navigate these things. I decided that I had to be direct about what had happened, and that I needed to come up with a plan so that I could show I bounced back from this obvious setback. I thought about my career goals, which were quite different from what I had been doing previously and decided that I had to do something now that was more connected to

my future goals. I felt this would really show that I was serious about my goals and that I could bounce back from this setback in a very positive way.

Although I obviously did not have much time to get my plan in action before submitting my application, I did take a few key steps and I did show my vision and overall plan. I actually think that my story turned out being better because of the layoff because instead of staying in a job that was not truly connected to my end goals, I had a new plan that bridged the gap and showed my initiative, as this new venture was something I did on my own (I did not go out and get a new job).

"I was laid off right before applying."

Anil
UC BERKELEY, HAAS

I was working in an industry in which there were tons of lay-offs in 2007, when I applied. My department had already gone through a few rounds of layoffs and I knew my time was coming. I felt that being laid off would look bad on my record and strongly considered resigning, so that this would all happen on my terms. When I started to think about this in the context of my MBA applications, I realized that I did not really have a good reason to resign. I had been at the company for a while, had progressed nicely, had survived several rounds of layoffs and my future goals were closely linked to my current role. Given the environment, it would be hard for

me to quit and then find a better job which could rationalize my actions. So, I decided to stay, and lo and behold was indeed laid off a few weeks later. It definitely took me a while to land on my feet. I ended up taking an internship in which I was not paid for a while and then eventually landed a similar job but for pay. These subsequent positions were somewhat distanced from the actual nuts and bolts of what I eventually wanted to do but they were with small companies so I gained a lot of hands-on experience in many different areas and higher level experience than I would get in a really big company. I was able to tell a pretty good story about this additional experience, and in general what I learned from being laid off.

"I turned my lay-off into a strength"

Munish
U MICHIGAN, ROSS

Being laid off just six months into my first job definitely wasn't a highlight in my career, and it was one of my biggest concerns in this application process. However, after my discussions with my admissions consultant, I was able to come up with a good strategy on how to handle it: just treat it as a fact that I was let go because of company downsizing and the economic slowdown after 9/11.

One of the biggest risks I took in my app was to highlight my lay-off—right in my career goals essay! I spun it around and showed it as a stepping stone. I paused because of the lay-off and assessed what was really important to me. Then I stepped into my new career building technologies that helped the disabled. Plus, I really showed my emotions about the lay-off and my new career goals.

I focused more on what I learned from the experience and how I grew personally and professionally. I was able to discuss it in essays dealing with constructive criticism, failures and disappointments…it ended up paying off pretty well! In fact, now that I think about it, I think I was a better business school candidate because I was laid off. I was able to show elements that I might not otherwise have been able to illustrate and my application was much stronger because of it.

The Essays: The Details

Style: Striking the Perfect Tone

CHAPTER 36

Confident, but Not Overconfident

It's all about "attitude." Your attitude will permeate your essays and set the tone for the way the admissions committee views you when you apply to a top-flight business school. When b-school aspirants sit down to actually craft their essays, they realize what a fine line they walk as they seek to develop their literary persona throughout the handful of required essays.

One of the key questions candidates have is: how confident should I try to appear? It's fun telling a story full of your achievements and peppered with remarks that show your confidence, pride, and skills. When you do this verbally to someone across a table from you, you are able to pick up on verbal and visual cues that let you know if you need to ratchet the confidence back one or two levels. With b-school essays, you have one shot to craft your message, and those passages will be read by people with diverse personality types and differing levels of acceptance and patience for bravado.

How do we highlight our business and leadership achievements without sounding like we are God's gift to Commerce? A couple of pointers:

- Acknowledge the team: NASCAR drivers use the "we" technique to a fault. "We were running great today. When we took that first turn, our car was running perfectly." You don't want to sound like a cliché, but positioning your achievements as team achievements works wonders. Plus, ultimately your abilities as a business leader will be more dependent on your abilities to achieve in a team format than in an individual setting.

- Balance your portfolio of essays: You probably have more license to highlight your truly impressive achievements when you gain credibility in other essays by being honest and open about failures, weaknesses, and doubts you have had. If you just highlighted how the incredible amounts of work you plowed into an entrepreneurial venture led it to be such a success, then you shouldn't in another essay half-heartedly chime in with "sometimes I work too hard" as a personal or professional weakness.

- Highlight mentors: If you are shining the spotlight on your leadership capabilities, make sure you also acknowledge people in your academic, extracurricular, or work settings from whom you learned some of these skills. This works equally well for "hard" skills (finance, negotiation, etc.) and "soft" skills (leadership, communications, ability to mentor, etc.). It shows you are good at acknowledging strengths in others and know how to learn from them.

Be Confident You Will Be a Valuable Classmate

Striking the right balance between confidence and humility is definitely one of the critical challenges you will face in crafting your b-school essays and in delivering answers to admissions interviewers. No one likes a blowhard…but, hey, no one else is going to "toot your horn" in your application.

Some applicants face a dilemma in how expert to paint themselves in their field. It is, indeed, critical to portray yourself as someone from whom your classmates can learn. Many business schools are case study–oriented; the quality of the education is essentially determined by the content the students contribute in the classroom. Additionally, "off-line" conversations are a huge part of the learning process for academic subjects as well as issues related to career choices.

However, the "I've seen it all approach" is definitely not what the b-schools are looking for from their typical 25- to

30-year-old applicant. Even as you highlight the fascinating experiences you've had and the cutting-edge knowledge you possess, make sure you take careful stock of what you want to learn, both in the classroom and from your fellow students. The people who take best advantage of business schools are those who come in with a high level of curiosity—an eagerness to be a sponge.

In short, the appropriate balance is struck when you have a developed and detailed awareness of what you have to teach and what you have to learn. You have a willingness and an ability to share your knowledge with others (which is very different from just having knowledge) and will be an active seeker of others' knowledge.

It's also important that folks who come from positions and industries lacking that "glamour" factor don't downplay their accomplishments. Certain high-profile investment banks and consulting firms are definitely the main "feeder" companies to American business schools, but it is often the people who come from less well-represented areas that have the most to teach the section or study group. When I entered business school in 1996, the top professional firms were definitely viewed as the place to be, but by the time I left in the late '90s, we all realized that people who had started the humblest of small businesses had a lot to teach us about potential entrepreneurial career paths. You may have run a T-shirt shack. Or conducted accounting audits for sketchy firms. Or monitored quality control at a Senegalese ball bearing plant. Rest assured, you do have valuable things to teach your classmates. The trick comes in smartly thinking through what those lessons are and showing you have an unusual perspective on them.

CHAPTER 38

What You Thought, Felt, Said, and Did

In recent years, MIT-Sloan's essay questions have included a bit of a unique wrinkle. In addition to asking you to describe your leadership experiences, accomplishments, and other managerial highlights, Sloan requested you recount "what you thought, felt, said and did."

Some MBA aspirants are perplexed and bewildered. They hate having to describe their innermost thought processes. Personally, I love it. I recommend that applicants take this approach to the essays for all of their schools. MBA programs are not looking for management automatons that are programmed from birth to calculate every NPV correctly and navigate every human resources crisis with aplomb. They realize young leaders are figuring it out as they go along. And this struggle makes for a more engaging story.

It's the Arnold Schwarzenegger approach vs. the Bruce Willis approach. Both are action heroes. Both kill their fair share of bad guys. Both have clever catch-phrases they utter throughout their adventures.

But all we know about Arnold is what he does. I mean, the man *literally* played an automaton in *Terminator*. Even where he's supposed to be a little bit more human, like in *Predator*, he barely shows a hint of fear. Bruce Willis, on the other hand, always makes mistakes on his way to saving the day. We see the momentary look of fear in his face before he strengthens his resolve and goes back to face the terrorists who took over Nakatomi Plaza. Bloody feet be damned!

Though the following is a bit of a simplistic example, I hope it illustrates the strength of the "thought, felt, said, and did" approach. A CliffsNotes version of a strong applicant's essay might read something like this:

> We contacted our largest customer to renegotiate our contract with them. We stressed the improvements in our product and our high levels of service as reasons why they should sign on for an even bigger order. They agreed and we expanded our deal.

Nice achievement, Arnold. Solid execution. But the story is a little more compelling if the reader can see behind the scenes.

> In spite of the risk I saw to our core business, we contacted our largest customer to renegotiate our contract with them. We stressed the improvements in our product and our high levels of service as reasons why they should sign on for an even bigger

order. It seemed like an eternity as we waited those few crucial minutes for them to analyze our proposal. But they agreed and we expanded our deal. We breathed a sigh of relief: our start-up would make payroll for another month.

Now, we know more about you and the context and importance of your achievement. Leaving space in your essays to delve into your thoughts and emotions will strengthen your credibility as a maturing future business leader.

Hasta la vista.

CHAPTER 39

Life's A Mystery, But Your Essays Shouldn't Be

know you're just trying to build some drama. You're trying to captivate the admissions committee reader. You're trying to enthrall, entice, and enrapture them with the flow of your story. But you shouldn't plan to construct your essays as an exercise in slow-building, crescendo-ing stories. You need to tell the reader what she is about to learn about you from the very beginning and then prove it to her point by point.

Some writers want to structure their essays as mysteries. The writer sets the stage by describing the dire circumstances the protagonist is facing. The protagonist then goes about overcoming every obstacle thrown in his or her way. And finally, all the pieces come together and our protagonist enjoys a tremendous success! (Or failure, in the case of some business school essays.)

MBA applicants need to reveal more at the very beginning, so the reader knows what to look for in the essay. Often, this means putting the moral of the story first:

For a **leadership** essay, this means writing, "My experience working at Smallco.com showed me that true leadership often means managing from below and questioning preconceived notions about how an organization should run."

NOT: "I joined Smallco.com because of the company's exciting approach to the fast-growing nanotechnology market."

For an **achievement** essay, this means writing, "Building a not-for-profit aid organization in the aftermath of the Southeast Asian tsunami was taxing, but it is by far my proudest achievement."

NOT: "When Sanjay prepared his fishing nets in the morning, he had no idea what the day had in store for him."

This doesn't mean that one has to sacrifice all elements of story-telling in the interest of creating a plain, flat-footed intro. First of all, the kind of accessible writing that makes for the clearest kind of introductions can still be engaging. Secondly, after introducing your readers to what they are about to learn about you, you can include more original storytelling formats. Those sentences about nanotechnology and Sanjay the fisherman are totally appropriate as the third or fourth sentence of a twenty-sentence essay; they still help set the tone near the beginning of your piece.

If you followed a mystery story approach, the good news is that there is often a quick fix. Sometimes, your conclusion can make an excellent intro. Just cut your ending couple of sentences that sum up the lessons learned and paste them at the front of the essay. You would be surprised how often this can work with minimal tweaking. If you have to choose between having a robust intro and a robust conclusion, go with the intro every time to engage your reader from the very beginning.

CHAPTER 40

Incorporating Humor

While **business school essays** should never attempt to reach "Borat" levels of comedy, MBA aspirants should look for opportunities to add some humor into their applications. As we've discussed before, MBA applications are not judged by machines, but by people who have to read a couple dozen of these things each day. Applications that incorporate a bit of well-placed humor are more entertaining and memorable for admissions readers.

If you believe that your sense of humor is one of the defining characteristics of "Brand You," this trait is best captured by demonstrating it rather than talking about it. A dull essay that lists sense of humor as a personal quality won't ring true.

The first rule when incorporating humor into b-school essays is "Less is More." You don't have room and readers don't have the patience for bits with long set-ups. We're not talking about jokes here; rather, the best kind of humor to incorporate falls more within the categories of the wry observation, the fond remembrance, or the honest portrayal of a confusing situation. Discussing the quirks of interesting and much loved characters who have impacted our lives can also make for an engaging essay.

In these cases, humor is not a silly gimmick. It's a way of capturing the truly humorous you.

The Nuts & Bolts

CHAPTER 41

"For Example...": Make It Real

Many applicants understand that, in theory, they need to fill their applications with colorful and interesting examples. So I wonder, why is the number one comment I make upon reading essays and letters of recommendation and conducting mock interviews— "Where are the examples?"

An essay claiming that you are a great leader, innovator, or team player may sound interesting. But it also sounds like you read the "how to get into b-school" book and just chimed in with the requisite buzzwords. Unless you can back up all of these claims, it is empty verbiage. The best way to convey your excellence is not through stating it, but through proving it with examples. Don't merely say it, show it!

Many of my clients start out thinking that they have not done anything that will really stand out. They have read friends' essays and do not think they have material that is nearly as impressive. However, as we discuss their background, we inevitably find interesting examples. A few years ago, one of my clients was stumped. He needed a good story for HBS question 1: "Describe a significant change that you brought about in an organization and its impact on your development as a leader." The example that we came up with was about revamping a monthly report at work. Not exactly a "save the world" kind of example. However, once written, it showed initiative, a desire to challenge the status quo, and an ability to execute and influence others. He also was able to articulate very specifically how it impacted the organization and helped him grow personally. The result? He went on to HBS.

It's important to realize that the strongest examples are not necessarily the "sexiest." A big M&A deal that landed in the *Wall Street Journal* may have gone by the book. But the smaller deal for a metal stamping business out of Milwaukee may have had more interesting strategic, interpersonal, or analytical challenges.

As you brainstorm examples for this year's apps, remember that even a simple example can be extremely effective. And without an example, it is almost not worth making a claim.

CHAPTER 42

One Question, Five Parts: Showing How the MBA Fits into Your Life

Wharton Question 1:

Describe your career progress to date and your future short-term and long-term career goals. How do you expect an MBA from Wharton to help you achieve these goals and why now?

Kellogg Question 1:

Briefly assess your career progress to date. Elaborate on your future career plans and your motivation for pursuing a graduate degree at the Kellogg School.

Harvard Question 6:

What are your career aspirations and how can an MBA help you to reach them? Why now?

Columbia Question 1:

What are your short-term and long-term post-MBA

goals? How will Columbia Business School help you achieve these goals?

This sort of questioning, from 2007 applications, can make you feel like Bill Murray in *Groundhog Day*!

All of these questions ask for the same general information, and yet all of them are very specific regarding what they want to know. Most questions in the career goals/why MBA category have several parts to them. Consider the Wharton question above; it is essentially five questions in one.

1. Describe your career progress to date.
2. Describe your future short-term goals.
3. Describe your future long-term goals.
4. How do you expect an MBA from Wharton to help you achieve these goals?
5. Why now?

The seemingly obvious rule of answering all parts of the question is often overlooked. In fact, I rarely read a first Wharton draft that clearly answers, "Why now?" On the flip side, I frequently review Harvard drafts that spend far too much time explaining, "Why Harvard." Harvard asks why you want an MBA, but not why specifically from Harvard.

A far too easy way to lose points on these essays is to not follow directions. When you neglect to answer parts of the question or when you answer pieces that are not there, you are not providing the information that is specifically being requested. Big mistake. Resist your urge to recycle identical essays from school to school (admissions can tell when you do that!) and make sure that you are tailoring your answers to the question being asked. As you approach an essay question, go through this simple exercise: break down the question as I have above. As you formulate ideas for the essay, check off which portion of the question is being answered. Make sure all parts are checked off in the end, and if your answer does not tie to the specific question, leave it out! These essay questions will change from year to year, but the approach to answering what is there and only what is there should remain constant.

CHAPTER 43

The Optimal Approach to the "Optional" Essay

When it comes to the optional essay offered by most schools, a frequent question is—is it really optional? Many applicants feel an obligation to write something, and struggle with what that something should be. Note that there are two different types of optional essays. In one scenario, the school will simply ask you to write about anything you feel is missing from your application that you would like them to know. This is the more flexible question. In the second situation, they are looking more specifically for gaps in work experience, or issues with your transcript or recommenders. In this scenario, they are looking for very specific information, and you should answer thoroughly but succinctly if you choose to answer at all.

In both cases, my approach to the optional essay is the following:

1) Complete your entire application, except for the

optional essay. Don't worry about that piece of the puzzle just yet.

2) Once complete, review your application and ask yourself if there is something extra you would like to communicate to the admissions committee.

3) If there is something missing, by all means, use the optional essay as an opportunity to say what you need to say!

4) If you cannot think of a topic you would like to cover, do not waste the admissions committee's time (or your time, for that matter).

I have seen a full range of topics for optional essays for the first scenario and frequently feel that the information included could have been incorporated elsewhere. When the optional essay is approached in this way, the applicant will take what could have been three lines of material and expand it into a full essay. This is a waste of everyone's time. Remember that the person reviewing your application has a lot of reading to do—so you want to make every word count. When brainstorming ideas for that optional essay, make sure that you cannot address the material elsewhere in the application. I frequently see the topic, "What I can contribute to your program." This is an example of a topic that really should be addressed all throughout your application, and often fits well into the primary essay about goals and program selection. As a result it feels superfluous and redundant when used for the optional essay.

In the second scenario described above you really need to be careful to follow their directions. The following is general advice and needs to be taken within the context of your overall strategy and the school that you are looking at. However, in *general*, the following topics are good material for this type of optional essay:

1) Explaining gaps in work experience.
2) Explaining choice of recommender.
3) Explaining extenuating circumstances affecting GPA, GMAT, or other aspects of your profile. This does not mean that you need to explain why you received a 3.5 one quarter as opposed to your usual 3.8. "Extenuating circumstances" means that something happened that significantly impacted your application. Perhaps there was a family crisis, or you were experiencing health problems. If your GPA dipped during this time, it would be very important for the admissions committee to know this.

To answer the question we began with: Yes, the optional essay is truly optional. So, exercise restraint!

Dealing with low grades

"I had an F on my transcript."

Javier
WHARTON

My GPA was consistently okay through college—definitely not stellar. However, at one point during my junior year, I actually failed a class. The F was pretty glaring on my transcript amidst lots of B's and some A's and C's, and I knew that I had to provide an explanation for the grade. I did have a pretty untraditional and challenging personal background. While I somewhat "escaped" my upbringing when I went off to college (the first in my family), there were definitely issues in my family that dragged me down. At one point, when I was dealing with some family issues, I completely lost track of my classes. In retrospect, I was emotionally not focused; I was really distracted. I also did not have the time to do my job which was financing my education, deal with my family issues and make several seven-hour car trips to be with my family, and study enough to do well. As a result, things really spiraled out of control in general but particularly with this one class, and I pretty much gave up on it and ended up failing.

This F played a part in my overall strategy in two ways. I spent one essay directly explaining the grade. All of the schools that I applied to had an optional essay for this type of thing so I wrote a brief, to-the-point essay explaining what was going on in my life during that time and how it

impacted my grades. I also discussed how my other classes in this subject matter (unfortunately it was a quantitative class so more relevant to business school) as well as my work experience, which was directly related to my goals, were evidence of my abilities and focus. The other issue was that my family and personal background, and my journey to even getting to college, was a significant part of my personal story in my MBA essays. So this extra "explanation" essay was really somewhat of an extension of that overall story. It was not a surprise within the context of the rest of the application. I guess they decided that one F was okay because I was admitted to two of my three top choices.

"My GMAT score offset low grades."

Sashi
UNIVERSITY OF VICTORIA, BC

My GPA was a concern to me, because I had gotten some very bad grades in some classes for a computer science major I was no longer excited about, but couldn't change. I received very high marks in business and other classes I took at university, however. I had feedback from Wharton that my low GPA within my major was originally a concern to them, but they felt I could handle the academic environment there since I received at 760 on the GMAT. I explained my low GPA in my essays—no other schools I got interviews with ever mentioned it. I had gotten into two excellent programs in INSEAD and NYU, but I basically chose U Vic because my new husband was here.

"I had a strong transcript with a glaring blemish."

Jim
WHARTON, CLASS OF 2008

I had a pretty strong GPA in a tough major from a very good school. I also had a graduate degree and had done very well there. My GMAT was solid, and I had a job that was quantitatively rigorous. My one blemish in this area was a C- in an economics course in undergrad. I prepared my applications assuming that the schools would realize that I was pretty strong academically and would not question this one little issue. I decided not to address it because I truly did not think it would matter and I did not want to bring more attention than necessary to it. I had my essays reviewed and more than one person suggested that I highlight the grade and explain what happened. The suggestion was that it was better for me to explain the background than for the schools to assume something about my abilities or attitude. So, I decided to prepare a very brief statement which did explain the situation and why I floundered during that semester. I discussed the personal circumstances behind the grade in about five sentences. I do not know if it was truly necessary to explain it. However, I do believe that if there is a question mark on the application that you can easily clear up, you might as well do so. The other thing that was positive was that discussing the circumstances actually revealed something more personal about me and in the end actually emphasized some positive aspects of my character. So for that reason alone, I was happy that I provided the explanation.

How to Wrap It Up

"Too Many Cooks in the Kitchen": Don't Let All That "Help" Turn into a Hindrance

As you head into the final stretch of the application process you may be tempted to take up the offer of every friend, family member, or co-worker who has volunteered to chip in his or her perspective on what makes the perfect essay.

Do not fall into this trap. It can lead to cluttered essays, garbled messages, and strained friendships. For every typo they catch, they could very well inject an extra dose of pain or complication into your process.

As addressed in Chapter 8, outside advisors can and should be a part of this MBA application process, don't get me wrong (c'mon, I wouldn't be writing all of this stuff if I didn't believe it). But this should be a very small circle of advisors. A professional advisor can be invaluable by helping set a "branding" strategy, by enforcing a schedule/process, and by judiciously editing essays in accordance with the "own work" standards laid out by business school admissions committees.

"Amateur advisors" are often employed by people who are not utilizing a professional advisor and even by some people who are. I recommend applicants not take on a horde of volunteers. True, many of these people may be showing their enthusiasm and belief in you by offering up their services, which is flattering—but a lot of these people might not be good writers or editors and may not have the necessary wisdom about the MBA application process. So, I recommend approaching one or two very trusted folks, people who have a very good sense of you as a person and know how to use the English language to good effect.

Instead of tapping into 30–60 minutes of free work time from four to six individuals (or more), get one or two people to invest four to six hours of their time over a multi-week period. They will be more knowledgeable about your overall strategy and your "brand" and this will be reflected in the applicability of their comments. If you approach this friend or colleague soon, he or she can be a guide over the next four weeks. You can make it worth their while: take them out to lunch or dinner during each feedback session.

With a horde of advisors, you may find yourself "chasing your tail," pursuing new sections and even new essays based on the whim of a person who read your essay on a crowded bus on the way to work. Don't get caught up in this. Employing just one or two well-briefed outside advisors will allow you to execute a more efficient process. At this stage of the game, you should be locking down on your essay topics and just working out ways to better explain the points you need to prove. Late December and early January is not the time to be questioning your approach based on a couple comments from Jim in accounting; rather, it's the time to slam home the points you've been working on and to accomplish your final polishing and proofreading.

SECTION VIII

Recommendations

Recommendations are an important and often overlooked aspect of your application. Many applicants don't concern themselves with the recommendations, incorrectly assuming that it is the responsibility of their selected recommender. Applicants often feel that if a recommendation is not terribly well written or is submitted a few days late, they will be excused, because it is their recommender's fault, not theirs! Applicants who do not prioritize the recommendations should consider this: you are going to business school to learn how to be a better manager. If you cannot manage something as simple as your own recommendations, what does that say about your management potential?

CHAPTER 45

Selecting the Right Recommenders

Workplace

Selecting the best recommender to write on your behalf is a critical first step in this very important aspect of the application process. All schools will detail what they are looking for in terms of a recommender and this may vary from school to school. For the most part, you will need at least two recommenders per school, with some asking for three. In general, your recommenders should be individuals who know you well from a work setting. Your primary recommender should be your supervisor. Almost all schools will want to hear from this individual with whom you interact frequently and who is responsible for managing you directly and can speak to your development, strengths, and weaknesses.

Beyond the supervisor, you can select one to two additional recommenders, again from a work setting or potentially from another setting in which you have demonstrated leadership. If you are not sure whether a recommender is appropriate, think about the types of questions he or she will have to answer. These questions are frequently linked to your leadership skills, your performance on teams, communication skills, ethics, and more. I often have clients who want to use a professor for a recommendation. A professor is usually not in a position to comment on these traits. If the recommender you are considering cannot say much more than "you are highly intelligent" or "you are a hard worker," he or she is probably not the right choice. However, you may decide to ask someone who has supervised you to some extent in an extracurricular setting. For example, if you have served on a board or done volunteer work for this individual's organization, he or she might be a perfect choice of someone who can comment on important skills from a different perspective, in a different setting.

I often have clients who are afraid to have multiple recommenders from a single job. This is not, in and of itself, a weakness. If you have had only one job this might be your only option and it is perfectly okay. In fact, if you have been at a job for more than two years, it might not make sense to go back and ask someone from your old job. The information a former employer would provide might not be current and provide a clear snapshot of who you are today. If you are asking recommenders from the same company, the key will be to ask individuals who can provide different perspectives. For example, in addition to your supervisor, you will ask the individual that you work with cross-functionally on a special project. Or you will ask the manager that you interact with as part of your recruiting efforts.

In addition to identifying the "right" people to write on your behalf, you need to use some intuition to determine whether these individuals will really do a great job. Consider the following questions:

1) Do your recommenders know you well?
2) Do you have a comfortable, productive relationship?
3) Do you feel they support your business school candidacy?
4) Do you have any reason to feel they might not write a positive recommendation?
5) Do they have the time to put in the effort and submit on time?
6) Do they write well?

Entrepreneurs

While you as an entrepreneur have a great story to tell in your essays, it can be very difficult to find an appropriate recommender, because you are your own boss. Clearly the supervisor position is not possible. Some options for the entrepreneur are:

- investor
- employee
- business partner
- board member
- mentor
- client
- strategic partner

You may also need to look outside of the business world for at least one of your recommenders. This is a time when it seems very fair to ask an individual from a non-career setting.

In the Family Business

If you work in a family business you may face essentially

the same challenge as an entrepreneur. If you are working for a parent or other family member, who can you ask to recommend you? Asking a family member of any kind is definitely not suggested, so similar to the entrepreneur you will have to be creative and think of other options. The suggested list for entrepreneurs is certainly a good place to start.

Prestigious Recommenders

Many applicants are tempted to ask their father's friend's friend who was president of a major public company…or a well known name that they have met in a social setting. The business schools have seen it all and will likely not be impressed by the fact that you are somehow connected to someone "important." It's a far better strategy to choose the individuals who conform to the criteria set forth above, who truly know you well and can comment honestly on important skills.

MBA Alums as Recommenders

It certainly does not hurt to have your recommendation written by an MBA, or even better, an alum from the school in question. If you are choosing between two recommenders who can write equally strong letters on your behalf, it would make sense to go with the alum. An alumnus can demonstrate a true understanding of what the program is looking for and state that you will be the right fit. Even an alum of a different program understands the type of person who will thrive in business school and so can speak with some authority regarding you as an applicant being a good fit. In general, the pedigree of your recommender is not entirely irrelevant. A letter from a VIP will have a greater impact, just as a high GPA from a prestigious school means more. All else being equal, feel free to go with the prominent alum or seasoned executive, but make sure that these people can truly talk about you, and you are not choosing them just for their resume. You should know that schools often make calls to recommenders to clarify a point or probe for additional information, so the recommender must be comfortable speaking about you.

CHAPTER 46

Recommendations: Don't Just "Hand Off," Strategize and Manage the Process

Once you identify potential recommenders, try to spend some "quality time" with these people—potentially even re-establishing ties with someone from a previous job or an old college prof—in order to feel out who would be most jazzed about writing a rec. Believe me, the recommender's attitude and commitment level are key.

Aim for a good "spread" among your recommenders, so they can write about you from various angles. Getting the partner from the "pharma cost-cutting consulting project" and also the partner from the "chemical cost-cutting consulting project" might not produce the recs that show the full range of your character and capabilities.

In general, I believe you should give these folks about six weeks of advance warning before the deadline and provide them any forms and prep materials three to four weeks before the date you would like the recommendation submitted.

This is no mere "hand-off," as some folks might believe. This is a task for which you should budget a few hours. All applicants need to figure out what their recs should say and how they should complement the points they themselves bring up in their essays. Even a recommender with the best intentions might end up writing a weak appraisal if it does not dovetail with the "Brand You" that is woven into your essays. For instance, a recommendation that emphasizes your data-gathering and quantitative analysis skills doesn't do much for you if you tried to establish your "brand" around creativity and dynamic leadership.

Provide your recommenders with a list of anecdotes that will jog their memories. Very specific anecdotes, like "Remember the time on the XYZ negotiation where you said the deal structure I proposed saved the company $10 million?" Some of these anecdotes or "micro-examples" can be ideas you yourself raise in the essays, while others might be fresh material that only the recommender employs.

CHAPTER 47

Don't Let Recommenders Become "Wreck-ommenders"

I **recently spoke with a** new client who believes poor recommendations were a key reason she was not admitted last year. She carefully selected her recommenders and gave them several months' advance notice. Her first recommender gave her a copy of his letter after submitting it. It was six pages long, written with care…and all wrong. He emphasized the wrong qualities, rambled like crazy, and did not provide relevant examples. Unfortunately, this is not uncommon—and it's the reason why managing your recommenders is as important as selecting the right ones.

The goal of managing your recommenders is to make it as easy as possible for them to write a glowing letter. The following process will also help you with your own essays, so it is a valuable exercise in and of itself.

1) Decide on four to five key characteristics that you would like your recommender to emphasize throughout the letter. Examples: leadership, team-

work, creative thinking, determination, focus, intelligence, charisma, integrity.

2) Come up with at least one concrete example that you feel illustrates each characteristic. Example: "Initiative—Last year, when I learned that international sales were declining, I took it upon myself to research the competitive landscape and learned of two recent market entrants. I then offered to lead a team to analyze these new competitors and develop a strategy for regaining our market share. Our team of five analysts proposed a solution after one week of work. The solution was implemented and within three months, we gained back 50% of lost market share."

3) Create a bullet pointed list of important projects that you have worked on, in more detail than your resume. You want your recommenders to actually read this document, so try to keep it to one page, and do not overload them with information. It should be a helpful, quick reference.

Invite your recommender to lunch and walk him or her through these materials. You should also provide a copy of your resume and discuss your goals. If possible, you can even share some of your essays with them. Don't leave it to your recommender to remember everything that you have done and don't leave this process to chance. Your recommenders will appreciate your assistance and thoroughness and will produce a better recommendation on your behalf.

CHAPTER 48

Extra Recommendations

Many applicants want to submit extra letters after the application has been submitted. They want to submit a letter from that VIP or someone very connected to the school who was not appropriate for an official letter of recommendation but could add an extra stamp of approval to the overall application, for example, a close family friend who knows you well in a social setting and is a prestigious alum of your target school. These letters need to be evaluated on a case-by-case basis. If done, they should come from the recommender and be submitted separately, after the application deadline, as an additional boost to your file. They should be brief and provide additional information—a truly new perspective on you.

Submitting extra recommendations is generally discouraged as the schools are barraged by these extra letters. However, in some cases it might make sense and you will need to evaluate it in the context of the individual, the school's policy, and the information that will be put forth in the letter. Some schools have more flexible policies than others. While it will be rare for a school to encourage additional letters, some take a much harder stand against them. If a school states that it does not want additional communication, take it seriously and think hard before sending them something that they say they do not want!

Interviews

CHAPTER 49

"STAR" Will Help You Shine in Interviews

When I was at Kellogg going through on-campus recruiting for my summer internship, I learned about an interview technique called the STAR method. I consider it to be one of the most useful frameworks for effectively answering interview questions and pass it on to all of my clients.

The STAR technique can be applied when asked "situational" questions.

"Tell me about a time you…"
- "Tell me about a time you failed."
- "Tell me about a time you came up with an innovative solution."
- "Tell me about a time you managed a difficult project."
- "Tell me about a time you led a team."

STAR stands for **S**ituation, **T**ask, **A**ction, **R**esult.

The power of the STAR method is that it allows you to formulate a very complete answer, but keeps your answer organized and keeps you from rambling on and on…a common occurrence in interviews.

For example:

Situation—"Product A was losing market share to a new competitor."

Task—"I needed to create a plan to regain our lost share."

Action—"I led a team to implement tactics A, B, and C."

Result—"We regained lost share, plus 10%."

And then you stop.

Try not to go longer than 90 seconds on any one answer. If you do, you may begin to see your interviewer's eyes glaze over. Often, the interviewer will probe further, asking for very specific details related to your story, so you need to be prepared. But just start with the basic elements of your story—STAR will help you get there.

CHAPTER 50

Common Interview Questions: Know Them, Nail Them

The interview is the most unpredictable portion of the application process. While it is important to prepare, it is virtually impossible to predict what you will be asked. Every interviewer is different and even the same person may differ depending on "mood" that day. That said, all you can do is your best, and there is a set of questions that you absolutely must be prepared for.

Make sure that you have outlined answers for the following questions:

- "Why do you want to go to business school?"
- "Why do you want to go now?"
- "What are your career goals?"
- "Why do you want to attend our program?"
- "Walk me through your resume."
- "Name three personal strengths and weaknesses."

Beyond that, you should have a handful of personal stories prepared. The questions should be flexible enough to serve as examples for a range of questions about teamwork, leadership, creativity, failure, facing challenges, and more. If you have this group of stories prepared and ready, you can access them as needed to answer any unpredictable situational questions that arise.

Once you have organized the content for your interviews and know the main points you want to make, make sure you practice out loud, in front of a mirror or with a friend. Don't assume that you can answer questions effectively just because you have written an essay on the topic and have outlined the answer in your head. My clients often schedule mock interviews feeling very confident and are surprised to find that their answers are disorganized, and that they ramble and go off track.

Remember that the goal of the interview is to discover more information about you, and only you are the expert here. However, to really come off as the expert you need to practice a bit. This does not mean that you should write down your answers word for word and memorize. It just means that you need to be comfortable speaking about yourself and telling your story. Since we do not normally engage in conversations where we spend 30 minutes talking about ourselves and rattling off accomplishments, it can take some practice to feel comfortable telling our story thoroughly yet succinctly.

Decisions

CHAPTER 51

Waitlist Agony, Waitlist Ecstasy

When you receive a waitlist notification, you are not quite sure how to feel. It is not an acceptance...and yet there is still hope. You are in agony—the waiting continues.

The first thing to do when you are waitlisted is congratulate yourself. While it probably is not the answer that you were hoping for, you should know that far more people are denied admission than placed on the waitlist. If you are waitlisted, you are still in the running, and your application has passed an important hurdle.

The waitlist has a lot of unknowns associated with it, even for the admissions committees. Until they know how many applicants will accept their invitations and until they start to understand the makeup of the class, they really do not know how many people will be admitted from the waitlist and who those people will be. In most cases, the waitlist is not technically ranked. Again, the admissions committee is looking at the class composition and trying to make sure that it is a well-rounded group. As their class begins to take shape, they can make more waitlist decisions.

While the waitlist may mean additional agony, it is usually an opportunity to further market yourself to the admissions committee. It is important to "follow the rules," so make sure you understand your school's waitlist policy. Some schools ask that you refrain from submitting additional materials, but most schools not only allow, but encourage, updates and additional information.

If additional materials are encouraged, what is appropriate? While each case is unique, the following is a list of things to consider:

1) Is your GMAT score below the school's average? If so, consider retaking the exam.

2) Did you make any contacts within the admissions committee? Now is the right time to reach out to these individuals and ask how you can improve your file or fill in any blanks.

3) Reiterate your interest in and commitment to the school through written communication.

4) Do you have someone who could write a recommendation and provide a new perspective on your abilities and personality?

5) If you have any changes to report related to personal or professional experiences, write a letter outlining these updates.

6) If you have not yet interviewed and an interview is offered, seize the opportunity!

The waitlist

"I got in off the waitlist!"

Jessica
KELLOGG

Kellogg was my absolute first-choice school. I was admitted to three other schools and even had a scholarship to one of them, but I desperately wanted to go to Kellogg because I truly felt it was the right fit for me. When I was waitlisted, I immediately came up with a plan to be in touch with the admissions committee on a fairly regular basis.

I started by writing them a letter that emphasized my desire to attend Kellogg. I struggled a bit with whether to tell them about the other acceptances, but ultimately left that out. I do not know if that was the right decision but it was what I decided to do. I just thought that it did not fit with the tone of the letter I was writing and I went with my gut feel regarding Kellogg's "culture." In the letter I also provided an update about my activities since I applied. I told them about a trip I had taken, an event I had helped to organize for a non-profit I volunteered for, and I also talked about my current deal at work. I tried to highlight a few aspects of my personality and activities.

My next step was to ask someone that I worked with in the non-profit to write a letter on my behalf. All of my other letters had been purely professional. My volunteer work was a significant aspect of my application, so I thought this would be a good opportunity to talk about my leadership in that setting. I know she submitted a pretty brief letter on my behalf.

I tried to check in monthly and I was in the middle of planning a letter from a current student when I was admitted! I am not saying that this is the magic formula to get in off of the waitlist, but I do think that if a school says they are interested in hearing from you then it certainly cannot hurt to check in on a fairly regular basis. I pretty much mapped out a monthly communication plan, which also helped me feel more in control of the situation. I did not ever call them or ask them what I should do, which might have been an idea as well. My strategy was more focused around keeping them updated on my level of interest and on my activities and less about filling in the holes because I truly thought that I had done everything I could up front.

CHAPTER 52

Deferrals

Every once in a while a new client and I will begin talking about application strategy and they will begin to show signs of uncertainty. They will bring up the possibility of waiting a year to apply…or applying this year and deferring if admitted. All schools have different policies on deferral, but they essentially fall into three camps.

Automatic Yes—I have been surprised to learn that some schools will automatically grant you a one-year deferral. No need for a big explanation, just let them know and you are granted one extra year. This is extremely rare!

Automatic No—Some schools will not allow deferrals. Never. No way. Don't bother asking because the answer will be no.

Maybe Yes, Maybe No—Most schools fall into this camp. If you find that you want or need to defer, call them and ask. They will consider your request and let you know. If your target schools fall into this camp, you should know that the bar for a "yes" is high. It is extremely difficult to be granted a deferral at most schools. A few years ago I had a client who was admitted to Wharton and Kellogg. Immediately after learning of the admits, his father was diagnosed as terminally ill. He called both schools and asked for deferrals, so that he could remain in Los Angeles and help care for his father. One school said yes, the other no.

If you are thinking about incorporating asking for a deferral into your strategy, this indicates that you are not ready to apply. While some situations, such as the one described above, are just unplanned, you must do your best to apply for the year you want to attend.

CHAPTER 53

Reapplications

Unfortunately, a mere 15% of applicants receive good news from some of the most competitive programs. If you are extremely focused and targeting only a small set of highly ranked programs, you may end up without any options at the end of the process—so you will need to contemplate reapplying the following year. Some schools are more friendly towards reapplicants than others. A reapplication can signal commitment to the MBA or to a particular school. If you are going to reapply, the key to a successful application will be demonstrating that you have learned, evolved, matured, and progressed since your prior application. For certain schools, reapplying the following year can be a difficult strategy because there is just not enough time to significantly improve your application. Other schools will see a more focused, mature application, an improved GMAT score, or a promotion at work, and that will be the difference they need in order to change their minds.

There are many ways to show that you have advanced. In your career, an obvious example is a promotion. But usually the promotions do not fall into place at exactly the time that we need. So you may have to create change in other ways. You may want to take a look around your office and think about processes or tools that can be improved upon. Then volunteer to be the one who makes the change. Or perhaps you would like to spearhead some morale-building activities or recruiting events, or lead community outreach programs. There are many small ways to emerge as a leader in your work environment. It is just up to you to find the opportunities and seize them.

Outside of work, the world truly is your oyster. If you are currently involved with activities or hobbies, think about how to grow into more of a leadership role and make an even bigger impact. If you do not have any "extracurricular" involvements, this is a great time to grow that aspect of your application.

Applicants will generally want to expand their list of schools when they reapply. I usually advise applicants to reapply to a school that they have their heart set on, but also to make some different choices. If there is a school that they are not terribly excited about or one that is just too competitive, perhaps it can be omitted in favor of new schools that are a better fit.

Reapplying

"I was a more well-rounded candidate."

Carl
UCLA, ANDERSON

The first time I was younger and more aggressive. I was less refined essentially. I didn't smooth out the edges…which was really representative of who I was as a person at the time. I was cognizant the second time of being more diplomatic.

My biggest challenge in reapplying was I felt that some of my best professional successes had come early in my career [with a dot-com start-up]. I thought the committee would perceive my early experiences as being of higher responsibility and more interesting. It was a challenge explaining what I had been doing in mortgages and consumer finance. Although I didn't feel the successes were of the same caliber, they were with a brand-name company the admissions committee had obviously heard of. But, I was a more mature candidate…potentially a better candidate the second time around.

I wanted to get a job with a company people had heard of…not a failed start-up. I wanted to work at a place with a known brand name, something they could wrap their brains around… something more conventional as opposed to entrepreneurial. I think it made a difference that I

had worked at places like HSBC and Wells Fargo. It might have made me look a little less like a "wild animal."

"My application was more focused the second time."

Edward
MIT, SLOAN

After I didn't get admitted to business school during my first attempt, I just figured I would go on without an MBA and just advance in my career. But then I saw at my work how people with MBAs were being promoted over similarly or better qualified candidates who didn't have MBAs. It was just a filter they used. That was kind of an eye opener. That more than anything else motivated me to apply again.

The first time I applied, I had no cohesive story. I basically said that I wouldn't really focus on the academics, but just get there and figure out what I want to do for the rest of my life. They don't want to hear that you won't care about the academics. They don't

want to hear that you'll be looking around at a bunch of things; they want to see a tight story. "I know exactly what I want to do and I know exactly what I want to get out of your school." They don't want to take the risk that someone is just going to wander around for a couple of years.

The best advice I got was to really focus in on a very specific story about myself. When they see Edward they need to say that "Edward is X, Y and Z." Very clearly, here are three things that I am and if they remember nothing else, they need to remember those three things.

You can't be a generic applicant, you need to stand out somehow. Whether you were a fighter pilot in Iraq or you spent time feeding kids in Africa, you can't just be the candidate who "hung out for four years and got some pretty good business experience under my belt." I think if you're going to get in, you have to have some niche the committee is looking to fill.

"I made sure my second app portrayed the 'real me.'"

Katie
UC BERKELEY, HAAS

I initially applied to Haas and put together an application that I thought was really strong. I put on my MBA hat and talked about the experiences on my resume, and my career goals. I knew that my numbers were a bit low, but I really felt I had high-quality work experience, and more experience than most applicants and I thought that would help me through. I asked my parents to review my application and they thought it was good too and sounded very professional. I had several friends at Haas at the time that I applied and I felt so comfortable there. I thought that I was a good "fit" for the school and was quite surprised when I was rejected, not even waitlisted.

At that point in time I was very ready to move on from my current job. I did not know what to do but I left my job and started doing design work independently. This was quite out of sync with my prior career moves, but it was what I was excited to do and I honestly did not think that I would be applying to school again. I had given it my best shot. A few months later I shared my application with a friend from Haas who gave me some really interesting feedback. She said that knowing me, she did not feel that the application reflected me at all. I had purposely left out some challenging personal experiences that I had gone through in the last few years, as well as some personal interests and activities. She advised me to reapply and take a different approach. I did not think about it too much, but two years later I did decide to apply. I was definitely above the average age by then and I was worried about submitting a reapplication that was extremely different from my initial application. However, I did just that. I was the same person, but discussed several personal experiences that had caused me to re-evaluate my goals and activities. This allowed me to explain my career transition and bring a more personal side to the application.

I think a lot of people are denied admission and then try to do a bunch of "right" things in order to improve their chances. In the years between my two applications I actually stopped doing

what I thought I "should" do, and started doing what I really wanted to do. The application that I submitted was much more genuine and reflected me. I knew that if I was not admitted I had truly put myself out there and given it my best shot. I think my application came off as pretty unique and had a lot of "heart." Of course I did keep in mind that this was a business school application and so really tried to address some of the issues that might concern them. For example, doing design work is not a typical pre-MBA job so I was careful to focus on managing the company, the engagements, the people that were working for me, and how much I had learned about running a business. I talked about how my goals had evolved since my last application, how I was more focused and in tune with what I really wanted to do. I definitely addressed my change of heart and tried to demonstrate how I had grown and developed in many ways, personally and professionally. This was an interesting learning experience for me because I do not consider myself to be a typical "MBA type." As a result, when I constructed my first application I was trying to fit into a certain mold and I really lost myself. The second time I was much more genuine (and interesting) and it worked! I was admitted to Haas, which was my first choice and waitlisted at Anderson (but withdrew).

Additional Aspects of Your Application

CHAPTER 54

The Resume

Most schools will ask that you submit a resume with your application. In almost all cases, this should be a one-page, professional resume, but it will likely be different from the resume you use when interviewing for a job. When you are interviewing for a job in IT, the prospective employer will want to learn all about your skills in coding, the programming languages you know, and technical processes with which you are familiar. A prospective business school will want to understand how you have led and worked in a team, and about your communication skills. Instead of rattling off the tactics of a given project, and writing in an industry-specific language that business school admissions committees might not even understand, you need to think hard about the broader skills developed on a given project. You will need to translate what you may feel are obvious aspects of delivering a project into a language that a business school admissions committee knows and about which they care.

The resume should be divided into three sections: Professional, Education, and Additional Information. The **Professional** section should be the bulk of the resume. You want to make sure that every point leads off with important action words such as "led," "delivered," and "created." This is in contrast to more passive and less colorful words such as "filed," "helped," and "worked." Each point should also be specific and results oriented, with quantifiable results whenever possible. For example, consider this entry on a resume:

> "Helped create new filing system"

Not particularly brag worthy? However, once transformed, it feels much more substantial:

> "Conceived of and implemented new office organizational system, which increased employee productivity and led to 24% savings in support costs."

The **Education** section of the resume should highlight college and graduate studies and generally should not go back to high school. You are considered an adult now and your high school studies will not be of interest. Their inclusion can make you appear immature.

The **Additional Information** section should be a brief one to three lines. It's a place to provide interesting items, such as hobbies, travel experience, and knowledge of foreign languages. This is where it is okay to have a line that reads, "Enjoy hiking, travel, and reading. Collect Pez dispensers." Often the additional information on your resume will serve as an ice breaker for the beginning of an interview, can convey a bit of color, and can be less formal.

Remember that anything on your resume is fair game for the interview. Be careful when you label your three years of high school Spanish as "fluent." You never know when the interviewer will decide to conduct your interview in Spanish "just for fun." Be prepared to speak intelligently and go into further detail on any of the bullet points. If any of the information is dated, go back and review and ensure accuracy before submitting.

CHAPTER 55

Data Forms

Don't underestimate the amount of time that your data forms can take. While they might appear to be insignificant compared to your essays, there is quite a bit of information stored in those forms and plenty of room for error. It's important to leave time to answer the questions thoroughly and carefully and then to recheck! While the forms generally do not leave much room for creativity, there is certainly a way to do them correctly and a way to stumble on these forms.

I do not recommend leaving the forms to the last minute. Throughout the process, you may find yourself burning out on essays and needing a break. This is the perfect opportunity to spend some time with your data forms. Make sure you return to them a couple of times to review in detail.

Ongoing Communications with Admissions Committees

Some applicants are able to form cordial relationships with members of an admissions committee. You may have traded business cards at a fairly intimate information session and followed up with a thank-you note. Or perhaps you interviewed on campus with an admissions representative and spent 30 minutes chatting together. Perhaps you called the office and connected with this individual who helped answer questions and was receptive to a follow-up email. These unplanned meetings can work to your advantage as you nurture these relationships. Keep in mind that even the warmest, most productive relationship will not "get you in" if your application is not strong. However, all things being equal, leaving a positive impression on an admissions representative or becoming a familiar and likable name cannot hurt. After all, these decision makers are only human.

The key to successfully developing these relationships

is to do so with care, and to remember that thousands of people are knocking on their doors every day. Keep correspondence brief, cordial, and relevant. Don't call or email just for the sake of it. Rather, ask a genuine question or communicate sincere appreciation. Don't waste their time with made-up questions—they will see right through it.

Too much contact

Omar
CORNELL

I think I would have gotten into Harvard if I had been more relaxed about the whole thing. I communicated with the admissions committee too much when I was on the wait list. There is definitely something called "too much" when it comes to talking with b-school admissions committees. I was calling them every other week and there were three different people I was talking to. I would recommend to people: Get noticed—and that's it. But I took it to the next level, and made it like it was a business transaction…following up all of the time. Someone from the adcom told me afterward basically that I would have gotten in if I wouldn't have been so over the top. Let the process run its course.

Conclusion

If you are reading this book, you have taken a solid first step in your business school admissions process. Some people will argue that the applications are harder than the curriculum. So, don't give up—business school will be a breeze if you can survive the grueling admissions process! As we said earlier, you should be prepared to struggle. The challenge is not so much about writing twenty essays, managing ten letters of recommendation, organizing interviews, school visits, transcripts, and more. The challenge is the process of reflection and introspection that can be terrifying and truly daunting. If done correctly, it can also be revealing and personally rewarding…not to mention exhilarating when you end up attending a dream school and hopefully altering the course of your life. In preparation for business school, here are some parting tips to consider as you embark on this great journey.

1) RECRUITING: Not long ago, most of your recruiters

were in your shoes—they are human. Be respectful, but don't be overly impressed. You should go to interviews and corporate presentations prepared to have a conversation and tell them about yourselves.

2) BROADENING YOUR EXPERIENCE: If you do not get involved with some activity outside of the classroom, you will not be reaping the full benefit of the MBA experience. There are a multitude of ways to get involved, and you will learn as much from these activities as you will from your studies. Activities will also help with you with networking and give you something to talk about in your interviews.

3) THE VALUE OF A BAD INTERNSHIP: While plenty of people go back to their summer employer, many do not. Even if you end up not enjoying your summer internship, it's still worthwhile to have the experience, and learn from it. Better to find out you don't like banking on an internship than on a full-time job. Do your best and know that no matter what happens, it is a valuable learning experience.

4) DON'T GIVE UP: Summer positions are often more competitive than full-time offers. If you are not able to land your dream internship, you still have a great chance at the same job full time.

5) STUDY HARD/PLAY HARD: A significant mode of learning will be from your fellow students. You will want to study hard and do your part to add your perspective. Taking your courses seriously is a good way to improve yourself, and to gain the respect of your classmates. However, be careful of isolating yourself and holing up in the library too long in pursuit of the perfect GPA. While studying and learning is important, you want to make sure you do not miss out on

other aspects of the experience. A successful student will be balanced and become involved outside of coursework.

6) REMEMBER YOUR VALUE: Your classmates will seem to be phenomenally accomplished, perhaps even intimidating. Don't forget that you, too, were accepted into the class for a reason. The school believes that you have a great deal to contribute, so make sure that you do.

7) HAVE AN OPEN MIND: Even if you are entering school with a firm idea of your career goals, use this time to explore a few options. Go to diverse corporate presentations, take classes in new subjects, interview with one company outside of your focus—you may be surprised.

8) PEOPLE UNLIKE YOU: You will probably gravitate to the "people like you," from the same country, with similar backgrounds. Your MBA class is an extremely diverse group. If you make an effort to get to know those outside of your comfort zone, your experience will be greatly enriched.

9) CREATE CHANGE: Not all, but most MBA programs are very flexible and constantly evolving. If you are dissatisfied with some aspect of the curriculum or programming, don't sit back and complain; instead, speak up and do something. Often you will be able to initiate a new class, a trip, a club, a conference, and more.

10) DON'T BURN BRIDGES: Remember that your classmates, whether you like them or not, are your professional network. Your class and the classes above and below you are all members of this priceless network. While you will want to relax, enjoy, and make friends,

always keep in mind that you may network with any of these people down the line.

Enjoy this experience—it's special and important. The application process is challenging, but can also help you to learn about yourself, make important decisions, improve in many ways, and hopefully put you on the road to an MBA from a great school that is the right fit for you.

Good luck!

About the Authors

Stacy **Sukov Blackman has** been consulting on the MBA application process since 2001, when she launched Stacy Blackman Consulting. She earned her MBA from the Kellogg Graduate School of Management at Northwestern University and her Bachelor of Science from the Wharton School at the University of Pennsylvania.

After graduating from Wharton, Stacy began working in finance at the Prudential Capital Group in San Francisco. Following business school, she transitioned into a career in marketing and has since worked in marketing roles at companies such as Charles Schwab, idealab! and Haagen Dazs. Through her work in marketing, Stacy identified similarities between traditional marketing and admissions strategy. She has developed a highly effective approach to marketing her clients successfully to top MBA programs.

In addition to private consulting, Stacy is a sought-after speaker on the topic of MBA admissions. She has coached alumni organizations at various schools and has run workshops at companies including JPMorgan, Lehman Brothers, UBS, and Credit Suisse First Boston. Stacy serves on the Board of Directors of AIGAC, the Association of International Graduate Admissions Consultants.

Stacy has been profiled in several publications, including *Fortune Magazine*, *BusinessWeek*, and the *Wall Street Journal*.

Since **his graduation from** the Harvard Business School, **Daniel J. Brookings** has worked as a strategy consultant. He has published many articles on strategy and marketing in major national business and technology periodicals. Since 2003, Daniel has advised scores of MBA applicants on how to create an effective personal branding strategy and craft compelling applications. Daniel is also an award-winning creative writer and has published a novel.